LINCOLN SPEECHES

ABRAHAM LINCOLN

EDITED WITH AN INTRODUCTION BY
ALLEN C. GUELZO

SERIES EDITOR
RICHARD BEEMAN

PENGUIN BOOKS

PENGUIN BOOKS
Published by the Penguin Group
Penguin Group (USA) Inc., 375 Hudson Street, New York, New York 10014, U.S.A.
Penguin Group (Canada), 90 Eglinton Avenue East, Suite 700, Toronto, Ontario,
Canada M4P 2Y3 (a division of Pearson Penguin Canada Inc.)
Penguin Books Ltd, 80 Strand, London WC2R 0RL, England
Penguin Ireland, 25 St Stephen's Green, Dublin 2, Ireland
(a division of Penguin Books Ltd)
Penguin Group (Australia), 250 Camberwell Road, Camberwell, Victoria 3124,
Australia (a division of Pearson Australia Group Pty Ltd)
Penguin Books India Pvt Ltd, 11 Community Centre, Panchsheel Park,
New Delhi - 110 017, India
Penguin Group (NZ), 67 Apollo Drive, Rosedale, Auckland 0632, New Zealand
(a division of Pearson New Zealand Ltd)
Penguin Books (South Africa) (Pty) Ltd, 24 Sturdee Avenue, Rosebank,
Johannesburg 2196, South Africa

Penguin Books Ltd, Registered Offices:
80 Strand, London WC2R 0RL, England

First published in Penguin Books 2012

5 7 9 10 8 6

Selection and book introduction copyright © Allen C. Guelzo, 2012
Series copyright © Richard Beeman, 2012
All rights reserved

Speeches from *The Collected Works of Abraham Lincoln,* in eight volumes and two
supplements, edited by Roy P. Basler, Marion Delores Pratt and Lloyd A. Dunlap,
published by the Abraham Lincoln Association.

LIBRARY OF CONGRESS CATALOGING IN PUBLICATION DATA
Lincoln, Abraham, 1809–1865.
[Speeches. Selections]
Lincoln speeches / Abraham Lincoln ; edited with an introduction by Allen C.
Guelzo.
p. cm.
"Penguin civic classics."
Includes bibliographical references.
ISBN 978-0-14-312198-5
1. Lincoln, Abraham, 1809–1865—Oratory. 2. United States—
Politics and government—1815–1861. 3. United States—Politics and
government—1861–1865. 4. Speeches, addresses, etc., American. I. Title.
E457.92 2012b
973.7092—dc23

2012022546

Printed in the United States of America
Set in Adobe Caslon · Designed by Sabrina Bowers

ALWAYS LEARNING   PEARSON

PENGUIN BOOKS

LINCOLN SPEECHES

ABRAHAM LINCOLN was born in a log cabin in Kentucky in 1809 and was largely self-educated. As his family moved to Indiana and then Illinois, he worked as a hired hand, clerk, and surveyor until, in his twenties, he began to study law. He was elected to the Illinois House of Representatives in 1834. After marrying Mary Todd, Lincoln set up his own law practice and was elected to the U.S. Congress in 1846. As a candidate for the U.S. Senate in 1858, he debated Senator Stephen A. Douglas across the state and became a national figure. Nominated for president by the Republican Party, Lincoln was elected in November 1860 and took office in March 1861. Commander in chief of the Union forces during the Civil War, he issued the Emancipation Proclamation in 1863. Reelected in 1864, Abraham Lincoln was shot to death by an embittered Southern actor, John Wilkes Booth, in April 1865, five days after General Lee's surrender at Appomattox.

ALLEN C. GUELZO is Henry R. Luce Professor of the Civil War Era and Director of Civil War Era Studies at Gettysburg College. He is the author of *Lincoln: A Very Short Introduction*, as well as two winners of the Lincoln Prize: *Lincoln's Emancipation Proclamation: The End of Slavery in America* and *Abraham Lincoln: Redeemer President*.

RICHARD BEEMAN, the John Welsh Centennial Professor of History Emeritus at the University of Pennsylvania, has previously served as the Chair of the Department of History, Associate Dean in Penn's School of Arts and Sciences, and Dean of the College of Arts of Sciences. He serves as a trustee of the National Constitution Center and on the center's executive committee. Author of seven previous books, among them *The Penguin Guide to the United States Constitution* and *Plain, Honest Men: The Making of the American Constitution*, Professor Beeman has received numerous grants and awards, including fellowships from the National Endowment for the Humanities, the Rockefeller Foundation, the Institute for Advanced Study at Princeton, and the Huntington Library. His biography of Patrick Henry was a finalist for the National Book Award.

CONTENTS

- ||||||||||||||||||||||||||||||||||||||||| -

SERIES
INTRODUCTION

We introduce the Penguin Civic Classics series by presenting our readers with a paradox. On the one hand, there is an abundance of evidence establishing that the vast majority of Americans, whatever their political differences, have an intense love of their country, believing that it has been one of the most successful experiments in human freedom and opportunity that the world has ever seen. And Americans are similarly united in having a deep reverence for their Constitution, for their institutions of government, and for the system of free enterprise that has been such a powerful engine for our economic growth. Americans see all of these as playing a vital role in making the nation as successful as it has been.

But there is an equally large body of evidence suggesting that Americans' knowledge of their history and of the way in which their institutions have worked over the course of that history is embarrassingly meager. For example, a third of Americans believe that the Declaration of Independence was written after the end of the Civil War, and fewer than half can identify the three branches of our federal government. Nearly 40 percent of the students at fifty-five of America's elite colleges and universities could not place the Civil War in the correct half century, and fewer than half of them, when presented with the text of the Gettysburg Address, were able to identify it. Nor does it appear that our knowledge improves much as we move closer to the present. Another survey has revealed that more than half of high school seniors thought that Italy, Germany, or Japan was a U.S. ally during the Second World War, and only 14 percent of those seniors could name any relevant fact about U.S. involvement in the Korean War. As the distinguished historian David McCullough has lamented, "While the clamorous popular culture races on, the American past is slipping away, out of sight and out of mind. We are losing our story, forgetting who we are and what it's taken to come this far."

With these discouraging results in front of us, it is no wonder that there is a growing clamor for an increased emphasis on "civic education," defined by one leading authority as "the cultivation of the virtues, knowledge, and skills" necessary for carrying out one's role as a citizen. That very phrase, "civic education," sounds to many like a doctor's prescription: "You need to take your medicine! It may not be very pleasant, but it is something you need to do in order to ensure not only your own health, but also the health of the body politic." It is our hope that reading these volumes in the Penguin Civic Classics series will be much more pleasant than taking medicine, for although these volumes will indeed help improve the reader's civic *knowledge*, we also hope that they will provide some civic *inspiration*—a genuine appreciation for, even an excitement about, some of the words, ideas, and actions that have shaped American society and government since their founding.

The history represented in these volumes, from the founding of the American colonies in the seventeenth century to the adoption of America's Declaration of Independence to Abraham Lincoln's inspiring Gettysburg Address to Barack Obama's inaugural address as the first African American president in American history, is not merely a collection of names and dates to be memorized but, rather, a set of stories to be absorbed and enjoyed. And they are stories that have a real relevance and meaning to our lives today, whether we are debating the nature of America's immigration laws, the extent to which the federal government should be involved in decisions relating to our health care, or, getting even closer to home, whether local schools and school districts have the constitutional right to search a student's school locker.

In these volumes, the reader will encounter nearly all of the central themes in American history, as well as the dilemmas and conflicts that have provided much of the dynamism and excitement of that history. The central themes and ideas of American public life—democracy, equality, economic opportunity, the role of government in maintaining that delicate balance between public order and personal freedom, and the government's responsibility to protect certain individual rights—have never remained static, nor have they ever elicited uniform agreement among American citizens.

The very first item in Terry Golway's collection of important American speeches is a sermon given by Massachusetts governor John Winthrop, aboard the ship *Arbella*, as it transported the first Puritan settlers to the new colony. In that sermon, Winthrop described the Puritans' mission in Massachusetts Bay as one of creating a "city upon a hill," a model of virtue and purity for all others in the world to follow. But his vision of that society was in some important respects very much at odds with the values that guide America today. In the opening words of his sermon, Winthrop reminded his fellow colonists that "GOD ALMIGHTY in His most holy and wise providence, hath so disposed of the condition of mankind, as in all times some must be rich, some poor, some high and eminent in power and dignity; others mean and in submission." Hardly a prescription for the democratic society that we claim to be today.

Fast-forward 136 years to the promise contained in Thomas Jefferson's Declaration of Independence that "all men are created equal"—a view of society *very* different from that articulated by Winthrop. Jefferson's city upon a hill was to be a nation dedicated to equality and the pursuit of happiness, not to a divinely ordained, inegalitarian social hierarchy. But, of course, in a world in which Africans were enslaved, women were considered legally subordinate to men and, indeed, in which many free white males were denied the right to vote because they did not own the requisite amount of property, Jefferson's promise of equality fell far short of an accurate description of the reality of American society in 1776. Still, words have power, and Abraham Lincoln, for one, knew the power of those words. As is amply displayed in Allen Guelzo's volume containing many of Lincoln's principal speeches, time and time again Lincoln invoked Jefferson's preamble as a pledge that Americans of his age were honor-bound to fulfill, describing the preamble as "the electric cord in that Declaration that links the hearts of patriotic and liberty-loving men together, that will link those patriotic hearts as long as the love of freedom exists in the minds of men throughout the world."

Alas, Americans would fight a horrific, bloody civil war in which more than 600,000 people, slave and free, lost their lives before the nation was able to take the steps necessary to forge the link to which Lincoln had referred. Beginning in December of 1865, with the adoption of the Thirteenth Amendment, eliminating the institution of slavery; continuing with the adoption of the Fourteenth Amendment (July 1868), with its guarantee of "equal protection under the laws"; and culminating with the adoption of the Fifteenth Amendment (February 1870), asserting that the right to vote could not "be abridged . . . on account of race, color, or previous condition of servitude," those ideas of democracy and equality began to be incorporated into our constitutional system. But although those three amendments represented an important step forward, America's struggle to live up to the promise of the preamble was far from over. It took until 1920 for the nation to adopt the Nineteenth Amendment, giving to women the right to vote, and in spite of the guarantees of the Fourteenth and Fifteenth Amendments, the civil rights of African Americans, including the right to vote, continued to be undermined by the actions of individual state governments well into the twentieth century. When Lyndon Johnson, only the second (after Woodrow Wilson) Southern-born president since the Civil War, signed into law the Voting Rights Act of 1965, he too quoted the preamble to the Declaration and ended his speech with a phrase from the anthem of the civil rights movement of the 1950s and 1960s: "We Shall Overcome." And when the first African American president, Barack Obama, delivered his inauguration speech on a cold day in January 2009, he began his speech by paraphrasing the words of Thomas Jefferson's preamble, urging Americans "to carry forward that precious gift, that noble idea, passed on from generation to generation: the God-given promise that all are equal, all are free, and all deserve a chance to pursue their full measure of happiness." Even in 2009 those words were, like Jefferson's, expressions of hope, not descriptions of reality. But they have proved powerful indeed, and they continue to be a dynamic force in shaping the American future just as they have the American past.

Another important theme that emerges from these volumes of Civic Classics involves the age-old debate on how and where to strike the best balance between public order and personal liberty. For most of human history, those who held government power—kings or emperors or czars—usually dealt with that issue by ruthlessly imposing their own definition of what was good for the masses of people whom they governed. When Thomas Paine published his earth-shaking pamphlet *Common Sense* in January of 1776, his primary purpose was to persuade the American colonists to throw off British rule, but one of the key elements in his argument was the notion that while every society needs some form of government in order to provide security and protect the freedom of its citizens, the best and freest societies are those in which government is least intrusive. In Paine's words: "Society in every state is a blessing, but government even in its best state is but a necessary evil; in its worst state an intolerable one." Paine's words struck a chord with his American readers, who were already suspicious of the overly powerful, distant government of Great Britain, and the Declaration of Independence, approved seven months later, reinforced that same theme. The distrust of concentrations of government power— the notion that government, while necessary, must be restrained—is deeply rooted in America's revolutionary past, and, of course, is very much alive today, as we can observe by the vitality of political movements such as the Tea Party.

As powerful as Paine's and Jefferson's indictments of excessive British power may have been, they did not provide the answer to the question of how the independent American nation could create a government that would strike an ideal balance between order and liberty. The men who gathered in Philadelphia in the summer of 1787 to frame a new constitution for their still-fragile independent nation took a giant step forward in providing an answer when they created a governmental system based on the division of power between the individual states and the central government—the system that we now call federalism—and by further dividing power among the three branches of the federal government— in a system that we characterize as one of "checks and balances."

But, as in so many other important ideas in American history, those involving federalism and checks and balances were subject to many different interpretations. Alexander Hamilton, James Madison, and John Jay, in the eighty-five essays comprising *The Federalist Papers*, attempted to address some of the concerns that Americans had about the excessive power of the proposed new federal government and, in the process, provided Americans with enduring insights about government and politics—insights that are still cited by Supreme Court justices in their judicial opinions even today. But Hamilton and Madison, the two principal authors of *The Federalist Papers*, began to disagree about the relationship of the new federal government to the individual states and to the people at large almost from the moment the new government commenced operation. The debate over the way the words of the Constitution should be interpreted, with Madison and Jefferson taking a "strict construction" position, and Hamilton, George Washington, and others arguing for a broader interpretation of the Constitution, has stayed with us until the present day. As readers of Jay Feinman's collection of landmark Supreme Court cases will discover, the Court has spent a significant portion of its time over the years, beginning with Chief Justice John Marshall's majority opinion in *McCulloch v. Maryland* (1819), wrestling with the extent of and limits on federal government power. Nor has that conflict been confined to judicial or intellectual arguments. In the years leading up to the Civil War, Northern and Southern politicians fought ferocious battles over the question of what authority the federal government had to legislate with respect to the expansion of slavery into new territories; once again, the ever-eloquent Abraham Lincoln weighed in on those issues, as is amply illustrated in Allen Guelzo's selection of Lincoln speeches. In the end, of course, it was not words that settled the constitutional argument between North and South but the force of arms. The Civil War was, in some senses, America's greatest civic failure, for knowledge and reason alone were not sufficient to settle the conflict between North and South. But however terrible the toll, it did resolve the paradox at the nation's core—the existence of the institution of slavery in a nation that claimed to be devoted to liberty.

Mercifully, the Civil War was the last occasion in which our differences of opinion over governmental power have resulted in warfare, but the war of words has never ceased. Whether debating issues relating to economic regulation, immigration, or providing and regulating health care, Americans—Republicans and Democrats, Tea Party members and Occupy Wall Street activists—

continue to differ, sometimes passionately, on the way our Constitution should be interpreted.

Americans, perhaps more than any other people in the world, have been ardently committed to defending their "rights." Indeed, when most Americans today think of their Constitution, they think not so much about those enumerated powers such as the levying of taxes, the regulating of commerce, or the coining of money that are contained in the main body of the Constitution, but, rather, they think of the "Bill of Rights." In fact, one of the few mistakes made by the framers of the Constitution in 1787 was their failure even to include a Bill of Rights in their final draft of the Constitution, a mistake that was, fortunately, remedied by the First Federal Congress in 1789. The rights articulated in our first ten amendments, including freedom of speech, the "free exercise of religion," freedom of the press, and freedom from unlawful search and seizure, have not only provided the foundation for the freedoms that we so value today but also have prompted some of our most vigorously debated controversies. Readers of Jay Feinman's volume on some of the most important Supreme Court decisions in our history will discover that, in general, the Court's definition of the rights guaranteed in those amendments has tended to widen over the course of our history. But there remain limits on the Bill of Rights protections enjoyed by Americans. For example, the right of free speech has not extended to public protests in which the threat of violence is imminent, and in an era of GPS tracking devices and CCTV cameras, Americans are confronted with new challenges in defining what constitutes an unlawful search and seizure.

The constitutional protection of individual rights has not been confined to those items specifically enumerated in the Bill of Rights. The Ninth Amendment, which says that the "enumeration in the Constitution, of certain rights, shall not be construed to deny or disparage others retained by the people," has been interpreted to include the right of privacy, including the right of a woman to have some control over her health and reproductive decisions. The best-known of the Supreme Court decisions relating to the right of a woman to terminate a pregnancy, *Roe v. Wade* (1973), far from settling that difficult question, has been followed by a series of subsequent Supreme Court decisions seeking to further refine and, in many cases, limit the right to obtain an abortion. The Court's decisions in these areas, far from being legal abstractions of interest only to a few history or civics teachers, have had an impact, and will continue to have an impact, on the lives of millions of women.

This series of Penguin Civic Classics is based on the belief that acquiring a knowledge of America's history and of our rights and responsibilities as citizens is not merely an abstract, academic exercise. *It really matters.* It can make a real difference in each and every one of our lives. And never more so than in the extraordinarily complicated, tumultuous, twenty-first-century world in which we live—a time of rapid, sometimes confounding, change. The historian David McCullough has spoken of the way in which our knowledge of history and of the way in which our institutions of government operate can give us a "sense of navigation, a sense of what we've been through in times past and who we are." It can also *empower* us. If we are familiar with the way in which people in the past have confronted their problems, and if we have a decent understanding of how to make the best use of America's institutions to deal with the problems confronting us in the present, we have a much better chance of being able to control our own destinies. Our opinions of the "correct" way to proceed may not always prevail, but we will at least be participants, not passive bystanders, in the ongoing drama that is the history of the United States. And, perhaps most important of all, it is often personally more rewarding, more fun, to be a participant rather than to be a bystander.

RICHARD BEEMAN

INTRODUCTION

Abraham Lincoln was not a naturally gifted speaker. His law partner of fourteen years, William Henry Herndon, remembered that "Lincoln's voice was, when he first began speaking, shrill, squeaking, piping, unpleasant." He had no formal education as a speaker—or much education at all, for that matter—and was wary of speaking off-the-cuff lest his rough-hewn mannerisms wear through the thin professional patina he had poured over them. On the night before his most famous speech, he declined a call for him "to make a speech" because "in my position it is somewhat important that I should not say any foolish things."[1]

And yet, no one in American political history stands taller as a maker of speeches than Abraham Lincoln. He was not the most attractive speaker, to judge by the first impressions he made on listeners. But he understood that, in the civic framework of a democracy, the art of speaking was a necessary component of popular government. "Our government rests in public opinion," Lincoln said in 1856. And how could it be otherwise (he explained in 1859), because "in a Government of the people, where the voice of all the men of the country, enter substantially into the execution—or administration, rather—of the Government—in such a Govern-

ment, what lies at the bottom of it all, is public opinion."
Within that framework, no one in American public life
gave clearer voice to the beauties of democracy, to
the supremacy of natural rights over social status, to the
moral foundations of politics, and to the practice of hu-
mility, perspective, and resilience as the hallmarks of
democratic leadership. And whatever Lincoln lacked in
grace and style as a speaker, he more than compensated
for it by his deployment of logic, commonly acknowledged authority, wit, and clarity, along with a natural
literary flair. Illinois judge David Davis (who presided
over the Eighth Judicial Circuit, where Lincoln practiced as a lawyer) rated Lincoln as "the best stump
speaker in the State." Even though Lincoln suffered
from "the want of an early education," he "has great
powers as a speaker," and another legal associate of many
years, Leonard Swett, warned that "any man who took
Abe Lincoln for a simple-minded man would soon
wake up with his back in a ditch."[2]

Lincoln's long suit as a speaker was not drama, but
persuasion. Mary Cunningham Logan, who heard Lincoln in his series of debates with Stephen A. Douglas in
1858, thought that Douglas "won your personal support
by the magnetism of his personality," but Lincoln
"seemed able to brush away all irrelevant matters of discussion, and to be earnestly and simply logical." Give
them each five minutes, and Douglas "would make the
greater impression." Give them an hour, "and the contrary would be true." For Lincoln, the key to this persuasion was clarity. He cultivated what the philologist
George Perkins Marsh called, in 1859, "the Saxon
element"—an "archaic" simplicity (similar to the King
James Bible and Shakespeare's plays), along with repeti-

tion and reformulation, parallelism and antithesis, and the use of proverbial formulas. "Lincoln always struggled to see the thing or the idea exactly and to express that idea in such language as to convey that idea precisely," Herndon recalled. He was, as John Todd Stuart (his first law partner) described him, "philosophical—logical—mathematical."[3]

What little training Lincoln could be said to have had in speaking came from five sources: his strongly Calvinistic family's memorization and recitation of the Bible, an early fascination with Shakespeare, the texts of political speeches printed in small-circulation newspapers and read aloud in community gatherings, the "readers" and "preceptors" that formed the bulk of schoolroom textbooks in America in the early nineteenth century, and the raw necessity of convincing juries. He had some practical preparation through participation in a "debating club" when he moved to New Salem, Illinois, in "1832 or 1833," and it was in 1832 that he gave what was probably his first political speech, as a candidate for the Illinois state legislature at "a sale of goods" in the now-defunct village of Papsville, Illinois:

> Gentlemen and Fellow-Citizens: I presume you all know who I am. I am humble Abraham Lincoln. I have been solicited by many friends to become a candidate for the legislature. My politics are short and sweet like the old woman's dance. I am in favor of a national bank. I am in favor of the internal improvement system and a high protective tariff. These are my sentiments and political principles. If elected, I shall be thankful; if not it will be all the same.[4]

But the most potent influence on Lincoln as a speaker was the political culture of the Whig Party, whose policies favoring a "national bank," the "internal improvement system," and "a high protective tariff" were Lincoln's banner all through his political career. The Whigs, organized in the 1830s by Henry Clay (whom Lincoln considered as his "beau ideal of a statesman"), were the party of middle-class entrepreneurs, as severely rational in their politics and speech as they were in economic calculation. It was the badge of Clay's Whigs to appeal, not to "the feelings and passions of our Countrymen," but "to their reasons and their judgment." This stood in rhetorical (as well as economic and political) contrast to the Democratic Party, whose figurehead in Lincoln's youth was the formidable Andrew Jackson. "Old Hickory" was unapologetic for his violence and coarseness of speech. Lincoln, in his search for precision, emotional restraint, and persuasive logic, would labor to act an entirely different political part. Even after the death of the Whig Party in the 1850s, and Lincoln's alignment with the new Republican Party, he continued to speak like "an old-line Henry Clay Whig."[5]

Lincoln never wrote a book. He dabbled in poetry and journalism, but almost all of what composes the standard collections of Lincoln's writings are either letters or speeches. But the boundary between his *writings* and *speeches* was a porous one. In many cases before his election to the presidency in 1860, the speeches are only transcripts taken down in a more or less haphazard fashion by newspaper reporters and editors who heard him speak, as they did in the campaign speech he delivered in Worcester, Massachusetts, in 1848, or his Lewistown, Illinois, speech on the Declaration of Independence. The great debates with Stephen A. Douglas in 1858 that made Lincoln nationally famous were unrehearsed and unscripted, but they were taken down with unusual precision in shorthand and published word for word in the Chicago newspapers within forty-eight hours.

But a number of what we regard as Lincoln's "speeches" were never actually spoken by him. His annual messages to Congress (what are now known as presidential "State of the Union" speeches) were not delivered before Congress, or anywhere else; they were sent in written form to the Senate and House of Representatives to be read by a clerk, and then printed by vote of Congress. On the other hand, some of what are characterized as Lincoln's writings were intended for delivery as speeches. The "public letter" he wrote to James Cook Conkling in 1863 was Lincoln's response to an invitation by Conkling (an old political friend and fellow lawyer in Springfield) to address a pro-administration "mass meeting" in Springfield. Nevertheless, he expected it to be read aloud to the rally, and instructed Conkling in exactly how he wanted it read. "You are one of the best public readers. I have but one suggestion. Read it very slowly." In fact, Conkling arranged to have it performed as a sort of political tableau, with another lawyer reading it aloud to Conkling, on the platform, with the rally's attendees as the audience.[6]

There are also several important statements of Lincoln's that may have been both written *and* spoken material. The 1837 protest against slavery, which he and Daniel Stone presented to the Illinois legislature, may have been read aloud and then submitted in writing, or simply the latter. His lengthy interview with John W. Crisfield on emancipation was certainly delivered orally to Crisfield alone, but with the expectation that Crisfield would, in turn, re-present those comments in approximately the same form to Congress (which Crisfield did) and then in print. Lincoln's "address" on colonization to a delegation of African American church pastors from the District of Columbia was evidently well rehearsed, but our only record of it is a lengthy newspaper summary—and yet, a summary that Lincoln was clearly expecting the newspapers to disseminate widely. His letter to Kentucky newspaper editor Albert Hodges in 1864 is actually Lincoln's own rehearsal of comments he delivered orally to Hodges and two others. Yet, Lincoln obviously intended that his letter should be circulated by Hodges in print as if it *had* been a speech—as in some senses it was.

Always wary of misstatement, Lincoln only infrequently spoke without notes, although one example of this seems to be the comments he made at Independence Hall on Washington's birthday in 1861. He had already made a set speech that morning, and the words he uttered outside at a flag-raising ceremony were probably spontaneous and unprepared. The responses Lincoln gave to "serenades" from groups of political well-wishers on the White House grounds also have the feel of being impromptu utterances. And yet it is hard to believe that, given their content, Lincoln had given no thought to them beforehand, so we have to assume that behind the utterance was something worked out on paper.

His greatest speeches were those for which he meticulously prepared written manuscripts beforehand. In his first "annual message" in 1861, he actually recycles substantial amounts of material from an address to the Wisconsin State Agricultural Fair in 1859. The great

Peoria speech of October 16, 1854, was a carefully structured affair, with fine attention to detail, and captures all of the themes that became salient to Lincoln's life in the 1850s and 1860s—his hatred of slavery, his fear that slavery was polluting the American commitment to democratic republicanism and the Declaration of Independence, and his conviction that the Kansas-Nebraska Act (and the doctrine of "popular sovereignty" that Stephen A. Douglas had written into it) would be the back channel by which slavery established itself in the new western territories. If everything else Lincoln wrote or said were somehow lost, the survival alone of this speech would allow us to reconstruct almost in full the shape of Lincoln's political thought: the clear commitment of the Founders to liberty, his "zeal" for protecting the example of the American democracy in an age dominated by monarchies, his determined evenhandedness, and his belief in a moral law that must undergird and surround politics.

Lincoln had, as the 1837 protest illustrates, always regarded slavery as an evil. But he had worked on the assumption that the intentions of the Founders (to which he appealed in the Cooper Union speech) and the provisions of the Missouri Compromise of 1820 (designed by Henry Clay) were both intended to secure the gradual extinction of slavery. The Kansas-Nebraska Act, as he demonstrated in the "House Divided" speech, was a rude awakening to the truth that slaveholders in the Southern states and their Democratic political allies in the North intended no such thing.

Little of Lincoln's animus against slavery was generated by any feeling of deep racial empathy for enslaved blacks, nor was he enthused about reform movements, especially those that demanded immediate implementation of absolute moral solutions without counting their cost (something he made clear in his speech to the Washington Temperance Society, in his Worcester speech in 1848, and in his eulogy for Henry Clay in 1852). Like Clay, he believed that a system of gradual emancipation, complete with paid compensation to slave owners and followed by colonization, was the most fitting "solution" to the black "problem." What Lincoln feared most about slavery was the threat it posed to white laborers, who would find themselves increasingly reduced to near-feudalism as a system of inflexible race-based labor fostered a similarly inflexible system of class immobility. And if there was one thing that Lincoln prized above all in American democracy, it was the open-ended opportunities for self-transformation offered by liberal capitalism—virtues that he was at pains to describe in his speeches in Milwaukee in 1859 and New Haven, Connecticut, a year later. But the hard experience of the Civil War taught him that few slaveholders—even in the northernmost "border states" where slavery was at its weakest—were willing to surrender even to gradual, compensated emancipation. At that point, he turned to military force to destroy slavery, opened service in the federal armies to freed slaves, and finally committed himself, as much as the presidency would legally allow, to civil equality for black Americans.

He never accepted the notion that the American Union was a loose confederation, bound only by self-interest, or the idea that democracy could survive free-will withdrawals whenever democratic decision making became difficult. His greatest fear for the future of the American republic, as far back as his speech on "The

Perpetuation of Our Political Institutions" in 1838, was that it would self-destruct, and his two "messages" to Congress in 1861 powerfully set out the case for the Civil War as "a people's contest," which would show that democracies really could protect themselves from internal disruption as readily as from outside invasion. At the summit of his eloquence, in the brief dedication remarks at the creation of the Soldiers National Cemetery at Gettysburg in November 1863, he was adamant that the war was not some petty political squabble, but a stress test of the durability of the very idea of popular government, or any government "dedicated to the proposition that all men are created equal." If the American republic could not hold together, then the whole democratic experiment would be called into question, just as the fall of the Berlin Wall sounded the knell for communism. The driving force behind the Gettysburg remarks, as well as so much else in Lincoln's speeches, was the peril posed to any democracy by a forgetfulness of the string of political values about equality, natural rights, and the ordinary competence of ordinary people to manage their own affairs that were the heart of a democratic order.

Yet, in the end, with victory in sight, Lincoln revealed no trace of vindictiveness. His second inaugural, delivered as the Confederate rebellion was finally expiring, was a surprisingly frank rebuke to anyone inclined to look upon the impending Northern triumph as some vindication of Yankee supremacy. Slavery was a crime for which all Americans had to answer, and the war was the penance imposed upon all. From the ashes of that purgatory, he insisted, must arise "malice toward none, charity for all." Five weeks later, he was dead from an assassin's bullet, and without his words as pillars of fire and cloud, there was an abundance of malice, and charity for only a very few. Still, in the record that remained, Lincoln had carved democracy's tables of stone. As Massachusetts senator Charles Sumner—often his opponent, frequently his critic, occasionally his friend—said, Lincoln had "made speeches that nobody else could have made. . . . Therefore, we honor him, & Fame takes him by the hand."[7]

ALLEN C. GUELZO

A NOTE ON THE TEXT

All but one of the texts of Lincoln's speeches and speaking in this collection are drawn from *The Collected Works of Abraham Lincoln*, in eight volumes and two supplements, edited by Roy P. Basler, Marion Delores Pratt, and Lloyd A. Dunlap, and published in 1953 by Rutgers University Press of New Brunswick, New Jersey. The sole exception is John Crisfield's account of his meeting (along with three other members of Congress) with Lincoln on March 10, 1862, as found on pages 210–211 in *The Political History of the United States of America, During the Great Rebellion, from November 6, 1860, to July 4, 1864*, edited by Edward McPherson and published in 1864 in Washington, DC, by Philp & Solomons.

All speeches and writings included in this volume are abridged except for "Protest Entered in the Illinois Legislature, Vandalia, Illinois, March 3, 1837"; "Address Delivered at the Dedication of the Cemetery at Gettysburg, November 19, 1863"; "Speech to the One Hundred Sixty-sixth Ohio Regiment, Washington, DC, August 22, 1864"; "Response to a Serenade, Washington, DC, February 1, 1865"; and "Second Inaugural Address, Washington, DC, March 4, 1865."

LINCOLN
SPEECHES

TO THE PEOPLE OF SANGAMO COUNTY,
NEW SALEM, ILLINOIS,
March 9, 1832

Fellow-Citizens: Having become a candidate for the honorable office of one of your representatives in the next General Assembly of this state, in accordance with an established custom, and the principles of true republicanism, it becomes my duty to make known to you—the people whom I propose to represent—my sentiments with regard to local affairs.

Time and experience have verified to a demonstration, the public utility of internal improvements. . . . With respect to the county of Sangamo, some more easy means of communication than we now possess, for the purpose of facilitating the task of exporting the surplus products of its fertile soil, and importing necessary articles from abroad, are indispensably necessary.

. . . No other improvement that reason will justify us in hoping for, can equal in utility the rail road. It is a never failing source of communication, between places of business remotely situated from each other. Upon the rail road the regular progress of commercial intercourse is not interrupted by either high or low water, or freezing weather, which are the principal difficulties that render our future hopes of water communication precarious and uncertain. Yet, however desirable an object the construction of a rail road through our country may be;

however high our imaginations may be heated at thoughts of it—there is always a heart-appalling shock accompanying the account of its cost, which forces us to shrink from our pleasing anticipations. The probable cost of this contemplated rail road is estimated at $290,000—the bare statement of which, in my opinion, is sufficient to justify the belief, that the improvement of Sangamo river is an object much better suited to our infant resources. . . . From my peculiar circumstances, it is probable that for the last twelve months I have given as particular attention to the stage of the water in this river, as any other person in the country. In the month of March, 1831, in company with others, I commenced the building of a flat-boat on the Sangamo, and finished and took her out in the course of the spring. Since that time, I have been concerned in the mill at New Salem. . . . From this view of the subject, it appears that my calculations with regard to the navigation of the Sangamo, cannot be unfounded in reason; but whatever may be its natural advantages, certain it is, that it never can be practically useful to any great extent, without being greatly improved by art. . . . I believe the improvement of the Sangamo river, to be vastly important and highly desirable to the people of this county; and if elected, any measure in the legislature having this for its object, which may appear judicious, will meet my approbation, and shall receive my support.

It appears that the practice of loaning money at exorbitant rates of interest, has already been opened as a field for discussion; so I suppose I may enter upon it without claiming the honor, or risking the danger, which may await its first explorer. It seems as though we are never to have an end to this baneful and corroding system, acting almost as prejudicial to the general interests of the community as a direct tax of several thousand dollars annually laid on each county, for the benefit of a few individuals only, unless there be a law made setting a limit to the rates of usury. A law for this purpose, I am of opinion, may be made, without materially injuring any class of people. . . .

Upon the subject of education, not presuming to dictate any plan or system respecting it, I can only say that I view it as the most important subject which we as a people can be engaged in. That every man may receive at least, a moderate education, and thereby be enabled to read the histories of his own and other countries, by which he may duly appreciate the value of our free institutions, appears to be an object of vital importance, even on this account alone, to say nothing of the advantages and satisfaction to be derived from all being able to read the scriptures and other works, both of a religious and moral nature, for themselves. For my part, I desire to see the time when education, and by its means, morality, sobriety, enterprise and industry, shall become much more general than at present, and should be gratified to have it in my power to contribute something to the advancement of any measure which might have a tendency to accelerate the happy period.

. . . But, Fellow-Citizens, I shall conclude. Considering the great degree of modesty which should always attend youth, it is probable I have already been more presuming than becomes me. However, upon the subjects of which I have treated, I have spoken as I thought. I may be wrong in regard to any or all of them; but holding it a sound maxim, that it is better to be only sometimes right, than at all times wrong, so soon as I discover my opinions to be erroneous, I shall be ready to renounce them.

Every man is said to have his peculiar ambition.[8] Whether it be true or not, I can say for one that I have no other so great as that of being truly esteemed of my fellow men, by rendering myself worthy of their esteem. How far I shall succeed in gratifying this ambition, is yet to be developed. I am young and unknown to many of you. I was born and have ever remained in the most humble walks of life. I have no wealthy or popular relations to recommend me. My case is thrown exclusively upon the independent voters of this county, and if elected they will have conferred a favor upon me, for which I shall be unremitting in my labors to compensate. But if the good people in their wisdom shall see fit to keep me in the background, I have been too familiar with disappointments to be very much chagrined. Your friend and fellow-citizen,

A. LINCOLN

PROTEST ENTERED IN THE ILLINOIS LEGISLATURE, VANDALIA, ILLINOIS, *March 3, 1837*

The following protest was presented to the House, which was read and ordered to be spread on the journals, to wit:

Resolutions upon the subject of domestic slavery having passed both branches of the General Assembly at its present session, the undersigned hereby protest against the passage of the same.

They believe that the institution of slavery is founded on both injustice and bad policy; but that the promulgation of abolition doctrines tends rather to increase than to abate its evils.

They believe that the Congress of the United States has no power, under the constitution, to interfere with the institution of slavery in the different States.

They believe that the Congress of the United States has the power, under the constitution, to abolish slavery in the District of Columbia; but that that power ought not to be exercised unless at the request of the people of said District.

The difference between these opinions and those contained in the said resolutions, is their reason for entering this protest.

DAN STONE,[9] A. LINCOLN,
REPRESENTATIVES FROM THE COUNTY OF SANGAMON.

"THE PERPETUATION OF OUR POLITICAL INSTITUTIONS," SPRINGFIELD, ILLINOIS, *January 27, 1838*

As a subject for the remarks of the evening, the perpetuation of our political institutions, is selected.

In the great journal of things happening under the sun, we, the American People . . . find ourselves in the peaceful possession, of the fairest portion of the earth, as regards extent of territory, fertility of soil, and salubrity of climate. We find ourselves under the government of a system of political institutions, conducing more essentially to the ends of civil and religious liberty, than any of which the history of former times tells us. We, when mounting the stage of existence, found ourselves the legal inheritors of these fundamental blessings. We toiled not in the acquirement or establishment of them—they are a legacy bequeathed us, by a once hardy, brave, and patriotic, but now lamented and departed race of ancestors. Theirs was the task (and nobly they performed it) to possess themselves, and through themselves, us, of this goodly land; and to uprear upon its hills and its valleys, a political edifice of liberty and equal rights; 'tis ours only, to transmit these, the former, unprofaned by the foot of an invader. . . .

How, then, shall we perform it? At what point shall we expect the approach of danger? By what means shall we fortify against it? Shall we expect some transatlantic military giant, to step the Ocean, and crush us at a blow? Never! All the armies of Europe, Asia and Africa combined, with all the treasure of the earth (our own excepted) in their military chest; with a Buonaparte for a commander, could not by force, take a drink from the Ohio, or make a track on the Blue Ridge, in a trial of a thousand years.

At what point then is the approach of danger to be expected? I answer, if it ever reach us, it must spring up amongst us. It cannot come from abroad. If destruction be our lot, we must ourselves be its author and finisher. As a nation of freemen, we must live through all time, or die by suicide.

I hope I am over-wary; but if I am not, there is, even now, something of ill-omen amongst us. I mean the increasing disregard for law which pervades the country; the growing disposition to substitute the wild and furious passions, in lieu of the sober judgment of Courts; and the worse than savage mobs, for the executive ministers of justice. . . . Accounts of outrages committed by mobs, form the everyday news of the times. They have pervaded the country, from New England to Louisiana—they are neither peculiar to the eternal snows of the former, nor the burning suns of the latter—they are not the creature of climate—neither are they confined to the slaveholding, or the non-slaveholding States.

. . . It would be tedious, as well as useless, to recount the horrors of all of them. Those happening in the State of Mississippi, and at St. Louis, are, perhaps, the most dangerous in example, and revolting to humanity. In the Mississippi case, they first commenced by hanging the regular gamblers: a set of men, certainly not following for a livelihood, a very useful, or very honest occupation; but one which, so far from being forbidden by the laws, was actually licensed by an act of the Legislature, passed but a single year before. Next, negroes, suspected of conspiring to raise an insurrection, were caught up and hanged in all parts of the State: then, white men, supposed to be leagued with the negroes; and finally, strangers, from neighboring States, going thither on business, were, in many instances, subjected to the same fate. Thus went on this process of hanging, from gamblers to negroes, from negroes to white citizens, and from these to strangers; till, dead men were seen literally dangling from the boughs of trees upon every road side; and in numbers almost sufficient, to rival the native Spanish moss of the country, as a drapery of the forest.

Turn, then, to that horror-striking scene at St. Louis. A single victim was only sacrificed there. His story is very short; and is, perhaps, the most highly tragic, of anything of its length, that has ever been witnessed in real life. A mulatto man, by the name of McIntosh,[10] was seized in the street, dragged to the suburbs of the city, chained to a tree, and actually burned to death; and all within a single hour from the time he had been a freeman, attending to his own business, and at peace with the world.

. . . But you are, perhaps, ready to ask, "What has this to do with the perpetuation of our political institutions?" I answer, it has much to do with it. . . . By such examples, by instances of the perpetrators of such acts going unpunished, the lawless in spirit, are encouraged to become lawless in practice; and having been used to no restraint, but dread of punishment, they thus become, absolutely unrestrained. Having ever regarded Government as their deadliest bane, they make a jubilee of the suspension of its operations; and pray for nothing so much, as its total annihilation. While, on the other hand, good men, men who love tranquility, who desire to abide by the laws, and enjoy their benefits, who would gladly spill their blood in the defense of their country; seeing their property destroyed; their families insulted, and their lives endangered; their persons injured; and seeing nothing in prospect that forebodes a change for the better; become tired of, and disgusted with, a Government that offers them no protection; and are not much averse to a change in which they imagine they have nothing to lose. Thus, then, by the operation of this mobocratic spirit, which all must admit, is now abroad in the land, the strongest bulwark of any Government, and particularly of those constituted like ours, may effectually be broken down and destroyed—I mean the attachment of the People. Whenever this effect shall be produced among us; whenever the vicious portion of population shall be permitted to gather in bands of hundreds and thousands, and burn churches, ravage and rob provision stores, throw printing presses into rivers, shoot editors,[11] and hang and burn obnoxious persons at pleasure, and with impunity; depend on it, this Government cannot last. . . . If the laws be continually despised and disregarded, if their rights to be secure in their persons and property, are held by no better tenure than the caprice of a mob, the alienation of their affections from the Government is the natural consequence; and to that, sooner or later, it must come.

Here then, is one point at which danger may be expected.

The question recurs, "How shall we fortify against it?" The answer is simple. Let every American, every lover of liberty, every well-wisher to his posterity, swear by the blood of the Revolution, never to violate in the least particular, the laws of the country; and never to tolerate their violation by others. As the patriots of seventy-six did to the support of the Declaration of Independence, so to the support of the Constitution and Laws, let every American pledge his life, his property, and his sacred honor—let every man remember that to violate the law, is to trample on the blood of his father, and to tear the charter of his own, and his children's liberty. Let reverence for the laws, be breathed by every American mother, to the lisping babe, that prattles on her lap—let it be taught in schools, in seminaries, and in colleges—let it be written in primers, spelling books, and in almanacs—let it be preached from the pulpit, proclaimed in legislative halls, and enforced in courts of justice. And, in short, let it become the political religion of the nation; and let the old and the young, the rich and the poor, the grave and the gay, of all sexes and tongues, and colors and conditions, sacrifice unceasingly upon its altars.

While ever a state of feeling, such as this, shall universally, or even, very generally prevail throughout the

nation, vain will be every effort, and fruitless every attempt, to subvert our national freedom.

When I so pressingly urge a strict observance of all
the laws, let me not be understood as saying there are no
bad laws, nor that grievances may not arise, for the re-
dress of which, no legal provisions have been made. I
mean to say no such thing. But I do mean to say, that,
although bad laws, if they exist, should be repealed as
soon as possible, still while they continue in force, for
the sake of example, they should be religiously observed.
So also in unprovided cases. If such arise, let proper legal
provisions be made for them with the least possible
delay; but, till then, let them if not too intolerable, be
borne with.

. . . But, it may be asked, why suppose danger to our
political institutions? Have we not preserved them for
more than fifty years? And why may we not for fifty
times as long?

We hope there is no sufficient reason. We hope all
dangers may be overcome; but . . . there are now, and
will hereafter be, many causes, dangerous in their tendency, which have not existed heretofore; and which
are not too insignificant to merit attention. That our
government should have been maintained in its original form from its establishment until now, is not much
to be wondered at. It had many props to support it
through that period, which now are decayed, and
crumbled away. Through that period, it was felt by
all, to be an undecided experiment; now, it is understood to be a successful one. Then, all that sought ce-
lebrity and fame, and distinction, expected to find
them in the success of that experiment. Their all was
staked upon it—their destiny was inseparably linked
with it. Their ambition aspired to display before an ad-

miring world, a practical demonstration of the truth of a proposition, which had hitherto been considered, at best no better, than problematical; namely, the capability of a people to govern themselves. If they succeeded, they were to be immortalized; their names were to be transferred to counties and cities, and rivers and mountains; and to be revered and sung, and toasted through all time. If they failed, they were to be called knaves and fools, and fanatics for a fleeting hour; then to sink and be forgotten. They succeeded. The experiment is successful; and thousands have won their deathless names in making it so. But the game is caught; and I believe it is true, that with the catching, end the pleasures of the chase. This field of glory is harvested, and the crop is already appropriated. But new reapers will arise, and they, too, will seek a field. It is to deny, what the history of the world tells us is true, to suppose that men of ambition and talents will not continue to spring up amongst us. And, when they do, they will as naturally seek the gratification of their ruling passion, as others have so done before them. The question then, is, can that gratification be found in supporting and maintaining an edifice that has been erected by others? Most certainly it cannot. Many great and good men sufficiently qualified for any task they should undertake, may ever be found, whose ambition would aspire to nothing beyond a seat in Congress, a gubernatorial or a presidential chair; but such belong not to the family of the lion, or the tribe of the eagle. What! think you these places would satisfy an Alexander, a Caesar, or a Napoleon? Never! Towering genius disdains a beaten path. It seeks regions hitherto unexplored. It sees no distinction in adding story to story, upon the monuments of fame, erected to the memory of others. . . . Is it unreasonable then to expect, that some man possessed of the loftiest genius, coupled with ambition sufficient to push it to its utmost stretch, will at some time, spring up among us? And when such a one does, it will require the people to be united with each other, attached to the government and laws, and generally intelligent, to successfully frustrate his designs.

. . . Another reason which once was; but which, to the same extent, is now no more, has done much in maintaining our institutions thus far. I mean the powerful influence which the interesting scenes of the Revolution had upon the passions of the people as distinguished from their judgment. By this influence, the jealousy, envy, and avarice, incident to our nature, and so common to a state of peace, prosperity, and conscious strength, were, for the time, in a great measure smothered and rendered inactive; while the deep rooted principles of hate, and the powerful motive of revenge, instead of being turned against each other, were directed exclusively against the British nation. . . . But this state of feeling must fade, is fading, has faded, with the circumstances that produced it.

. . . At the close of that struggle, nearly every adult male had been a participator in some of its scenes. The consequence was, that of those scenes, in the form of a husband, a father, a son or a brother, a living history was to be found in every family. But those histories are gone. They can be read no more forever. They were a fortress of strength; but, what invading foe-men could never do, the silent artillery of time has done; the levelling of its walls. . . . They were the pillars of the temple of liberty; and now, that they have crumbled away, that temple must fall, unless we, their descendants, supply their places with other pillars, hewn from the solid quarry of sober reason. Passion has helped us; but can do so no more. It will in future be our enemy. Reason, cold, calculating, unimpassioned reason, must furnish all the materials for our future support and defense.

SPEECH ON THE SUB-TREASURY, SPRINGFIELD, ILLINOIS,
December 26, 1839

Fellow-Citizens: It is peculiarly embarrassing to me to attempt a continuance of the discussion, on this evening . . . of . . . the Sub-Treasury scheme[12] of the present Administration, as a means of collecting, safe-keeping, transferring and disbursing the revenues of the Nation, as contrasted with a National Bank for the same purposes. Mr. [Stephen A.] Douglass[13] has said that we (the Whigs), have not dared to meet them (the Locos),[14] in argument on this question. I protest against this assertion. I assert that we have again and again, during this discussion, urged facts and arguments against the Sub-Treasury, which they have neither dared to deny nor attempted to answer. But lest some may be led to believe that we really wish to avoid the question, I now . . . lay down the following propositions, *to wit*:

1st. It will injuriously affect the community by its operation on the circulating medium.

2d. It will be a more expensive fiscal agent.

3d. It will be a less secure depository of the public money.

To show the truth of the first proposition, let us take

a short review of our condition under the operation of a National Bank. It was the depository of the public revenues. Between the collection of those revenues and the disbursements of them by the government, the Bank was permitted to, and did actually loan them out to individuals, and hence the large amount of money annually collected for revenue purposes, which by any other plan would have been idle a great portion of time, was kept almost constantly in circulation. Any person who will reflect, that money is only valuable while in circulation, will readily perceive, that any device which will keep the government revenues, in constant circulation, instead of being locked up in idleness, is no inconsiderable advantage.

By the Sub-Treasury, the revenue is to be collected, and kept in iron boxes until the government wants it for disbursement; thus robbing the people of the use of it, while the government does not itself need it, and while the money is performing no nobler office than that of rusting in iron boxes. The natural effect of this change of policy, every-one will see, is to reduce the quantity of money in circulation.

. . . Again, by the Sub-Treasury scheme the revenue is to be collected in specie.[15] . . . Now mark what the effect of this must be. By all estimates ever made, there are but between 60 and 80 millions of specie in the United States. The expenditures of the Government for the year 1838, the last for which we have had the report, were 40 millions. Thus it is seen, that if the whole revenue be collected in specie, it will take more than half of all the specie in the nation to do it. By this means more than half of all the specie belonging to the fifteen million of souls, who compose the whole population of the country, is thrown into the hands of the public office-holders, and other public creditors, composing in number, perhaps not more than one-quarter of a million; leaving the other fourteen millions and three-quarters to get along as they best can, with less than one-half of the specie of the country, and whatever rags and shin-plasters they may be able to put, and keep, in circulation. . . . In all candor, let me ask, was such a system for benefiting the few at the expense of the many, ever before devised? And was the sacred name of Democracy, ever before made to endorse such an enormity against the rights of the people?

I have already said that the Sub-Treasury will reduce the quantity of money in circulation. This position is strengthened by the recollection, that the revenue is to be collected in specie, so that the mere amount of revenue is not all that is withdrawn, but the amount of paper circulation that the 40 millions would serve as a basis to, is withdrawn; which would be in a sound state at least 100 millions. When 100 millions, or more, of the circulation we now have, shall be withdrawn, who can contemplate, without terror, the distress, ruin, bankruptcy and beggary, that must follow.

. . . It is often urged that . . . a National Bank produces greater derangement in the currency, by a system of contractions and expansions, than the Sub-Treasury would produce in any way. In reply, I need only point . . . to the period intervening between the time that the late Bank got into successful operation and that at which the Government commenced war upon it, to show that during that period, no such contractions or expansions took place.

. . . I now leave the proposition as to the effect of the Sub-Treasury upon the currency of the country, and pass to that relative to the additional expense which must be incurred by it over that incurred by a National Bank, as a fiscal agent of the Government. By the late National Bank, we had the public revenue received, safely kept, transferred and disbursed, not only without expense, but we actually received of the Bank $75,000 annually for its privileges, while rendering us those services. By the Sub-Treasury, according to the estimate of the Secretary of the Treasury . . . these services, under the Sub-Treasury system, cannot cost less than $600,000. . . . It is sufficient to pay the pensions of more than 4,000 Revolutionary Soldiers, or to purchase a 40-acre tract of Government land, for each one of more than 8,000 poor families.

I now come to the proposition, that it would be less secure than a National Bank, as a depository of the public money. The experience of the past, I think, proves the truth of this. . . .

By the Sub-Treasury scheme, the public money is to be kept, between the times of its collection and disbursement, by Treasurers of the Mint, Custom-house officers, Land officers, and some new officers to be appointed in the same way that those first enumerated are. Has a year passed since the organization of the Government, that numerous defalcations have not occurred among this class of officers? . . . But turn to the history of the National Bank in this country, and we shall there see, that those Banks performed the fiscal operations of the Government through a period of 40 years, received, safely kept, transferred, disbursed, an aggregate of nearly five hundred millions of dollars; and that, in all that time, and with all that money, not one dollar, nor one cent, did the Government lose by them. Place the public money again in a similar depository, and will it not again be safe? . . . Public officers, selected with reference to their capacity and honesty (which by the way, we deny is the practice in these days), stand an equal chance, precisely, of being capable and honest, with Bank officers selected by the same rule. . . . The Saviour of the world chose twelve disciples, and even one of that small number, selected by superhuman wisdom, turned out a traitor and a devil. And, it may not be improper here to add, that Judas carried the bag—was the Sub-Treasurer of the Saviour and his disciples.

We then, do not say, nor need we say, to maintain our proposition, that Bank officers are more honest than Government officers, selected by the same rule. What we do say, is, that the interest of the Sub-Treasurer is against his duty—while the interest of the Bank is on the side of its duty. . . . A Sub-Treasurer has in his hands one hundred thousand dollars of public money; his duty says—"You ought to pay this money over"—but his interest says, "You ought to run away with this sum, and be a nabob the balance of your life." And who that knows anything of human nature, doubts that, in many instances, interest will prevail over duty, and that the Sub-Treasurer will prefer opulent knavery in a foreign land, to honest poverty at home? But how different is it with a Bank? Besides the Government money deposited with it, it is doing business upon a large capital of its own. If it proves faithful to the Government, it continues its business—if unfaithful, it forfeits its charter, breaks up its business, and thereby loses more than all it can make by seizing upon the Government funds in its possession. Its interest, therefore, is on the side of its duty—is to be faithful to the Government, and consequently, even the dishonest amongst its managers, have no temptation to be faithless to it. But it is said, and truly too, that there is to be a Penitentiary Department to the Sub-Treasury. This, the advocates of the system will have it, will be a "king-cure-all."[16] Before I go farther, may I not ask if the Penitentiary Department, is not itself an admission that they expect the public money to be stolen?

. . . As a sweeping objection to a National Bank, and consequently an argument in favor of the Sub-Treasury as a substitute for it, it often has been urged, and doubtless will be again, that such a bank is unconstitutional. . . . Whatever objection ever has or ever can be made to the constitutionality of a bank, will apply with equal force in its whole length, breadth and proportions to the Sub-Treasury. Our opponents say, there is no express authority in the Constitution to establish a Bank, and therefore a Bank is unconstitutional; but we, with equal truth, may say, there is no express authority in the Constitution to establish a Sub-Treasury, and therefore a Sub-Treasury is unconstitutional. . . . Our position is that both are constitutional. The Constitution enumerates expressly several powers which Congress may exercise, superadded to which is a general authority "to make all laws necessary and proper," for carrying into effect all the powers vested by the Constitution of the Government of the United States. . . . Upon the phrase "necessary and proper," in the Constitution, it seems to me more reasonable to say, that some fiscal agent is indispensably necessary; but, inasmuch as no particular sort of agent is thus indispensable, because some other sort might be adopted, we are left to choose that sort of agent, which may be most "proper" on grounds of expediency.

. . . I know that the great volcano at Washington, aroused and directed by the evil spirit that reigns there, is belching forth the lava of political corruption, in a current broad and deep, which is sweeping with frightful velocity over the whole length and breadth of the land, bidding fair to leave unscathed no green spot or living thing, while on its bosom are riding like demons on the waves of Hell, the imps of that evil spirit, and fiendishly taunting all those who dare resist its destroying course, with the hopelessness of their effort; and knowing this, I cannot deny that all may be swept away. Broken by it, I, too, may be; bow to it I never will. . . . But, if after all, we shall fail, be it so. We still shall have the proud consolation of saying to our consciences, and to the departed shade of our country's freedom, that the cause approved of our judgment, and adored of our hearts, in disaster, in chains, in torture, in death, we *never* faltered in defending.

ADDRESS TO THE WASHINGTON TEMPERANCE SOCIETY, SPRINGFIELD, ILLINOIS, *February 22, 1842*

Although the Temperance cause has been in progress for near twenty years, it is apparent to all, that it is, *just now*, being crowned with a degree of success, hitherto unparalleled. . . . That that success is so much greater now than heretofore, is doubtless owing to rational causes; and if we would have it to continue, we shall do well to enquire what those causes are. The warfare heretofore waged against the demon of intemperance, has . . . not been the most proper. . . . Too much denunciation against dram-sellers and dram-drinkers was indulged in. This, I think, was both impolitic and unjust. It was *impolitic*, because, it is not much in the nature of man to be driven to anything; still less to be driven about that which is exclusively his own business; and least of all, where such driving is to be submitted to, at the expense of pecuniary interest, or burning appetite.

When the dram-seller and drinker, were incessantly told, not in the accents of entreaty and persuasion, diffidently addressed by erring man to an erring brother; but in the thundering tones of anathema and denunciation, with which the lordly judge often groups together all the crimes of the felon's life, and thrusts them in his face just ere he passes sentence of death upon him . . . it is not wonderful that they were slow, *very slow*, to acknowledge the truth of such denunciations, and to join the ranks of their denouncers, in a hue and cry against themselves.

To have expected them to do otherwise than as they did—to have expected them not to meet denunciation with denunciation, crimination with crimination, and anathema with anathema, was to expect a reversal of human nature, which is God's decree, and never can be reversed. When the conduct of men is designed to be influenced, *persuasion*, kind, unassuming persuasion, should ever be adopted. . . . If you would win a man to your cause, *first* convince him that you are his sincere friend. . . . On the contrary, assume to dictate to his judgment, or to command his action, or to mark him as one to be shunned and despised, and he will retreat within himself, close all the avenues to his head and his heart; and tho' your cause be naked truth itself, transformed to the heaviest lance, harder than steel, and sharper than steel can be made, and tho' you throw it with more than Herculean force and precision, you shall no more be able to pierce him, than to penetrate the hard shell of a tortoise with a rye straw.

. . . On this point, the Washingtonians greatly excel the temperance advocates of former times. Those whom they desire to convince and persuade, are their old friends and companions. *They* know they are not demons, nor even the worst of men. *They* know that generally, they are kind, generous and charitable, even beyond the example of their more staid and sober neighbors. *They* are practical philanthropists; and they glow with a generous and brotherly zeal, that mere theorizers are incapable of feeling.

. . . But I have said that denunciations against dram-sellers and dram-drinkers, are *unjust* as well as impolitic. Let us see.

I have not enquired at what period of time the use of intoxicating drinks commenced; nor is it important to know. It is sufficient that to all of us who now inhabit the world, the practice of drinking them, is just as old as the world itself. . . . When all such of us, as have now reached the years of maturity, first opened our eyes upon the stage of existence, we found intoxicating liquor, recognized by everybody, used by everybody, and repudiated by nobody. . . . It is true, that even *then*, it was known and acknowledged, that many were greatly injured by it; but none seemed to think the injury arose from the *use* of a *bad thing*, but from the *abuse* of a *very good thing*.

. . . If, then, what I have been saying be true, is it wonderful, that *some* should think and act *now*, as *all* thought and acted *twenty years ago*? And is it *just* to assail, *contemn*, or despise them, for doing so? The universal sense of mankind, on any subject, is an argument, or at least an *influence* not easily overcome.

. . . Another error, as it seems to me, into which the old reformers fell, was, the position that all habitual drunkards were utterly incorrigible, and therefore, must be turned adrift, and damned without remedy, in order that the grace of temperance might abound to the temperate *then*, and to all mankind some hundred years *thereafter*. There is in this something so repugnant to humanity, so uncharitable, so cold-blooded and feeling-less, that it never did, nor ever can enlist the enthusiasm of a popular cause. . . . It looked so fiendishly selfish, so like throwing fathers and brothers overboard, to lighten the boat for our security—that the noble minded shrank from the manifest meanness of the thing.

. . . By the Washingtonians, this system of consigning the habitual drunkard to hopeless ruin, is repudiated. *They* adopt a more enlarged philanthropy. . . . *They* teach hope to all—despair to none. As applying to *their* cause, *they* deny the doctrine of unpardonable sin. . . . To these *new champions*, and this *new* system of tactics, our late success is mainly owing; and to *them* we must chiefly look for the final consummation.

. . . Ought *any*, then, to refuse their aid in doing what the good of the *whole* demands? Shall he, who cannot do *much*, be, for that reason, excused if he do *nothing*? "But," says one, "what good can I do by signing the pledge? I never drink even without signing." This question has already been asked and answered more than millions of times. Let it be answered once more. For the man to suddenly, or in any other way, to break off from the use of drams, who has indulged in them for a long course of years, and until his appetite for them has become ten or a hundred-fold stronger, and more craving, than any natural appetite can be, requires a most powerful moral effort. . . . When he casts his eyes around him, he should be able to see, all that he respects, all that he admires . . . kindly and anxiously pointing him onward;

and none beckoning him back, to his former miserable "wallowing in the mire."[17] . . . Let us make it as unfashionable to withhold our names from the temperance pledge as for husbands to wear their wives' bonnets to church, and instances will be just as rare in the one case as the other.

. . . If the relative grandeur of revolutions shall be estimated by the great amount of human misery they alleviate, and the small amount they inflict, then, indeed, will this be the grandest the world shall ever have seen. Of our political revolution of '76, we all are justly proud. It has given us a degree of political freedom, far exceeding that of any other of the nations of the earth. In it the world has found a solution of that long mooted problem, as to the capability of man to govern himself. In it was the germ which has vegetated, and still is to grow and expand into the universal liberty of mankind. . . . And what a noble ally this, to the cause of political freedom. With such an aid, its march cannot fail to be on and on, till every son of earth shall drink in rich fruition, the sorrow quenching draughts of perfect liberty. Happy day, when, all appetites controlled, all passions subdued, all matters subjected, *mind*, all conquering *mind*, shall live and move the monarch of the world. Glorious consummation! Hail fall of Fury! Reign of Reason, all hail!

And when the victory shall be complete—when there shall be neither a slave nor a drunkard on the earth—how proud the title of that *Land*, which may truly claim to be the birthplace and the cradle of both those revolutions, that shall have ended in that victory. How nobly distinguished that People, who shall have planted, and nurtured to maturity, both the political and moral freedom of their species.

This is the one hundred and tenth anniversary of the

birthday of Washington. We are met to celebrate this day. Washington is the mightiest name of earth—*long since* mightiest in the cause of civil liberty; *still* mightiest in moral reformation. On that name, a eulogy is expected. It cannot be. To add brightness to the sun, or glory to the name of Washington, is alike impossible. Let none attempt it. In solemn awe pronounce the name, and in its naked deathless splendor, leave it shining on.

SPEECH ON THE WAR WITH MEXICO, WASHINGTON, DC,
January 12, 1848

Some, if not all the gentlemen on the other side of the House, who have addressed the committee within the last two days, have spoken rather complainingly, if I have rightly understood them, of the vote given a week or ten days ago, declaring that the war with Mexico was unnecessarily and unconstitutionally commenced by the President.[18] . . . I am one of those who joined in that vote; and I did so under my best impression of the *truth* of the case. How I got this impression, and how it may possibly be removed, I will now try to show. When the war began, it was my opinion that all those who, because of knowing too *little*, or because of knowing too *much*, could not conscientiously approve the conduct of the President, in the beginning of it, should, nevertheless, as good citizens and patriots, remain silent on that point, at least till the war should be ended. Some leading democrats, including ExPresident [Martin] Van Buren, have taken this same view, as I understand them; and I adhered to it, and acted upon it, until since I took my seat here; and I think I should still adhere to it, were it not that the President and his friends will not allow it to be so. Besides the continual effort of the President to argue every silent vote given for supplies, into an endorsement of the justice and wisdom of his conduct . . . the President, in his first war message of May 1846, declares that the soil was *ours* on which hostilities were commenced by Mexico; and he repeats that declaration, almost in the same language, in each successive annual message, thus showing that he esteems that point, a highly essential one. In the importance of that point, I entirely agree with the President. To my judgment, it is the *very point*, upon which he should be justified, or condemned.

. . . Now I propose to try to show, that the whole of this,—issue and evidence—is, from beginning to end, the sheerest deception. . . . My way of living leads me to be about the courts of justice; and there, I have sometimes seen a good lawyer, struggling for his client's neck, in a desperate case, employing every artifice to work round, befog, and cover up, with many words, some point arising in the case, which he *dared* not admit, and yet could not deny. Party bias may help to make it appear so; but with all the allowance I can make for such bias, it still does appear to me, that just such, and from just such necessity, is the President's struggle in this case.

Sometime after my colleague (Mr. [William] Richardson) introduced the resolutions I have mentioned, I introduced a preamble, resolution, and interrogatories, intended to draw the President out, if possible, on this hitherto untrodden ground.[19] To show their relevancy, I propose to state my understanding of the true rule for ascertaining the boundary between Texas and Mexico.

It is, that *wherever* Texas was *exercising* jurisdiction, was hers; and *wherever* Mexico was *exercising* jurisdiction, was hers; and that *whatever* separated the actual exercise of jurisdiction of the one, from that of the other, was the true boundary between them. If, as is probably true, Texas was exercising jurisdiction along the western bank of the Nueces, and Mexico was exercising it along the eastern bank of the Rio Grande, then *neither* river was the boundary; but the uninhabited country between the two, was. The extent of our territory in that region depended, not on any *treaty-fixed* boundary (for no treaty had attempted it) but on revolution.[20] Any people anywhere, being inclined and having the power, have the *right* to rise up, and shake off the existing government, and form a new one that suits them better. This is a most valuable,—a most sacred right—a right, which we hope and believe, is to liberate the world. Nor is this right confined to cases in which the whole people of an existing government, may choose to exercise it. Any portion of such people that *can*, *may* revolutionize, and make their *own*, of so much of the territory as they inhabit.

. . . As to the country now in question . . . all Mexico, including Texas, revolutionized against Spain; and still later, Texas revolutionized against Mexico. In my view, just so far as she carried her revolution, by obtaining the *actual*, willing or unwilling, submission of the people, *so far*, the country was hers, and no farther. Now sir, for the purpose of obtaining the very best evidence, as to whether Texas had actually carried her revolution, to the place where the hostilities of the present war commenced, let the President answer the interrogatories, I proposed, as before mentioned, or some other similar ones. . . . If he *can* not, or *will* not do this—if on any pretense, or no pretense, he shall refuse or omit it, then

I shall be fully convinced, of what I more than suspect already, that he is deeply conscious of being in the wrong—that he feels the blood of this war, like the blood of Abel, is crying to Heaven against him. That originally having some strong motive—what, I will not stop now to give my opinion concerning—to involve the two countries in a war, and trusting to escape scrutiny, by fixing the public gaze upon the exceeding brightness of military glory—that attractive rainbow, that rises in showers of blood—that serpent's eye, that charms to destroy—he plunged into it, and has swept, *on* and *on*, till, disappointed in his calculation of the ease with which Mexico might be subdued, he now finds himself, he knows not where.

SPEECH ON THE 1848 PRESIDENTIAL RACE, WASHINGTON, DC, *July 27, 1848*

Our democratic friends seem to be in great distress because they think our candidate for the Presidency don't suit *us*. Most of them cannot find out that Gen: [Zachary] Taylor [Whig candidate for President in 1848] has any principles at all. . . . They are in utter darkness as to his opinions on any of the questions of policy which occupy the public attention. But is there any doubt as to what he will *do* on the prominent questions, if elected? Not the least. . . . On the prominent questions of currency, tariff, internal improvements, and Wilmot Proviso,[21] Gen: Taylor's course is at least as well defined as is Gen: [Lewis] Cass' [Democratic candidate for President]. . . . We see it; and to us it appears like principle, and the best sort of principle at that—the principle of allowing the people to do as they please with their own business.

. . . Almost half the democrats here, are for [internal] improvements; but they will vote for Cass, and if he succeeds, their votes will have aided in closing the doors against improvements. Now this is a process which we think is wrong. We prefer a candidate, who, like Gen: Taylor, will allow the people to have their own way, regardless of his private opinions; and I should think the internal improvement democrats, at least, ought to prefer such a candidate. He would force nothing on them which they don't want, and he would allow them to have improvements, which their own candidate, if elected, will not.

. . . I am a Northern man, or rather, a Western free state man, with a constituency I believe to be, and with personal feelings I know to be, against the extension of slavery. As such, and with what information I have, I hope and *believe*, Gen: Taylor, if elected, would not veto the Proviso. *But* I do not *know* it. Yet, if I knew he would, I still would vote for him. I should do so, because, in my judgment, his election alone, can defeat Gen: Cass; and because, *should* slavery thereby go to the territory we now have, just so much will certainly happen by the election of Cass; and, in addition, a course of policy, leading to new wars, new acquisitions of territory and still further extensions of slavery. One of the two is to be President; which is preferable?

. . . But I suppose I cannot reasonably hope to convince you that we have any principles. The most I can expect, is to assure you that we think we have, and are quite contented with them. . . . But the gentleman from Georgia[22] further says we have deserted all our principles, and taken shelter under Gen: Taylor's military coat-tail; and he seems to think this is exceedingly degrading. Well, as his faith is, so be it unto him. But can he remember no other military coat tail under which a certain other party have been sheltering for near a quarter of a century? Has he no acquaintance with the ample military coat tail of Gen: [Andrew] Jackson? Does he not know that his own party have run the five last Presidential races under that coat-tail? and that they are now running the sixth, under the same cover? Yes sir, that coat tail was used, not only for Gen: Jackson himself; but has been clung to, with the gripe of death, by every democratic candidate since. You have never ventured, and dare not now venture, from under it. Your campaign papers have constantly been "Old Hickories" with rude likenesses of the old general upon them; hickory poles, and hickory brooms, your never-ending emblems; Mr. Polk himself was "Young Hickory," "Little Hickory" or something so; and even now, your campaign paper here, is proclaiming that Cass and [Democratic vice-presidential candidate William O.] Butler are of the true "Hickory stripe." No sir, you dare not give it up.

Like a horde of hungry ticks you have stuck to the tail of the Hermitage[23] lion to the end of his life; and you are still sticking to it, and drawing a loathsome sustenance from it, after he is dead. A fellow once advertised that he had made a discovery by which he could make a new man out of an old one, and have enough of the stuff left to make a little yellow dog. Just such a discovery has Gen: Jackson's popularity been to you. You not only twice made President of him out of it, but you have had enough of the stuff left, to make Presidents of several comparatively small men since; and it is your chief reliance now to make still another.

. . . There is one entire article of the sort I have not discussed yet; I mean the military tail you democrats are now engaged in dovetailing onto the great Michigander. Yes sir, all his biographers (and they are legion) have him in hand, tying him to a military tail, like so many mischievous boys tying a dog to a bladder of beans. True, the material they have is very limited; but they drive at it, might and main. He invaded Canada without resistance, and he *out*vaded it without pursuit. As he did both under orders, I suppose there was, to him, neither credit or discredit in them; but they constitute a large part of the tail. He was not at Hull's surrender,[24] but he was close by; he was volunteer aid to Gen: [William Henry] Harrison on the day of the battle of the Thames[25]; and, as . . . Harrison was picking huckleberries two miles off while the battle was fought, I suppose it is a just conclusion with you, to say Cass was aiding Harrison to pick huckleberries. This is about all, except the mooted question of the broken sword.[26] Some authors say he broke it, some say he threw it away, and some others, who ought to know, say nothing about it. Perhaps it would be a fair historical compromise to say, if he did not break it, he didn't do anything else with it.

By the way, Mr. Speaker, did you know I am a military hero? Yes sir; in the days of the Black Hawk war,[27] I fought, bled, and came away. Speaking of Gen: Cass' career, reminds me of my own. I was not at Stillman's defeat,[28] but I was about as near it, as Cass was to Hull's surrender; and, like him, I saw the place very soon afterwards. It is quite certain I did not break my sword, for I had none to break; but I bent a musket pretty badly on one occasion. If Cass broke his sword, the idea is, he broke it in desperation; I bent the musket by accident. If Gen: Cass went in advance of me in picking huckleberries, I guess I surpassed him in charges upon the wild onions. If he saw any live, fighting Indians, it was more than I did; but I had a good many bloody struggles with the musquetoes; and, although I never fainted from loss of blood, I can truly say I was often very hungry. Mr. Speaker, if I should ever conclude to doff whatever our democratic friends may suppose there is of black cockade federalism about me, and there-upon, they shall take me up as their candidate for the Presidency, I protest they shall not make fun of me, as they have of Gen: Cass, by attempting to write me into a military hero.

CAMPAIGN SPEECH FOR ZACHARY TAYLOR, WORCESTER, MASSACHUSETTS, SEPTEMBER 12, 1848

. . . Mr. Lincoln then passed to the subject of slavery in the States, saying that the people of Illinois agreed entirely with the people of Massachusetts on this subject, except perhaps that they did not keep so constantly thinking about it. All agreed that slavery was an evil, but that we were not responsible for it and cannot affect it in States of this Union where we do not live. But, the question of the *extension* of slavery to new territories of this country, is a part of our responsibility and care, and is under our control. In opposition to this Mr. L. believed that the self-named "Free Soil"[29] party, was far behind the Whigs. Both parties opposed the extension. . . . The "Free Soil" men in claiming that name indirectly attempted a deception, by implying the Whigs were *not* Free Soil men. In declaring that they would "do their duty and leave the consequences to God," merely gave an excuse for taking a course that they were not able to maintain by a fair and full argument.

To make this declaration did not show what their duty was. If it did we should have no use for judgment, we might as well be made without intellect, and when divine or human law does not clearly point out what is our duty, we have no means of finding out what it is by using our most intelligent judgment of the consequences. . . .

EULOGY ON HENRY CLAY,
SPRINGFIELD, ILLINOIS,
July 6, 1852

On the fourth day of July, 1776, the people of a few feeble and oppressed colonies of Great Britain, inhabiting a portion of the Atlantic coast of North America, publicly declared their national independence, and made their appeal to the justice of their cause, and to the God of battles, for the maintenance of that declaration. That people were few in numbers, and without resources, save only their own wise heads and stout hearts. Within the first year of that declared independence, and while its maintenance was yet problematical—while the bloody struggle between those resolute rebels, and their haughty would-be masters, was still waging, of undistinguished parents, and in an obscure district of one of those colonies, Henry Clay was born. The infant nation, and the infant child began the race of life together. For three quarters of a century they have travelled hand in hand. They have been companions ever. The nation has passed its perils, and is free, prosperous, and powerful. The child has reached his manhood, his middle age, his old age, and is dead. In all that has concerned the nation the man ever sympathized; and now the nation mourns for the man.

. . . Throughout that long period, he has constantly been the most loved, and most implicitly followed by friends, and the most dreaded by opponents, of all living American politicians. In all the great questions which have agitated the country, and particularly in those great and fearful crises, the Missouri question—the Nullification question, and the late slavery question,[30] as connected with the newly-acquired territory, involving and endangering the stability of the Union, his has been the leading and most conspicuous part. . . . It is probably true he owed his preeminence to no one quality, but to a fortunate combination of several. He was surpassingly eloquent; but many eloquent men fail utterly; and they are not, as a class, generally successful. His judgment was excellent; but many men of good judgment, live and die unnoticed. His will was indomitable; but this quality often secures to its owner nothing better than a character for useless obstinacy. These then were Mr. Clay's leading qualities. No one of them is very uncommon; but all taken together are rarely combined in a single individual; and this is probably the reason why such men as Henry Clay are so rare in the world.

Mr. Clay's eloquence did not consist . . . of types and figures—of antithesis, and elegant arrangement of words and sentences; but rather of that deeply earnest and impassioned tone, and manner, which can proceed only from great sincerity and a thorough conviction, in the speaker of the justice and importance of his cause. This it is, that truly touches the chords of human sympathy; and those who heard Mr. Clay, never failed to be moved by it, or ever afterwards, forgot the impression. All his efforts were made for practical effect. He never spoke merely to be heard. He never delivered a Fourth of July Oration, or a eulogy on an occasion like this. As a politician or statesman, no one was so habitually careful to avoid all sectional ground. Whatever he did, he did for the whole country. In the construction of his measures he ever carefully surveyed every part of the field, and duly weighed every conflicting interest. Feeling, as he did, and as the truth surely is, that the world's best hope depended on the continued Union of these States, he was ever jealous of, and watchful for, whatever might have the slightest tendency to separate them.

Mr. Clay's predominant sentiment, from first to last, was a deep devotion to the cause of human liberty—a strong sympathy with the oppressed everywhere, and an ardent wish for their elevation. With him, this was a primary and all controlling passion. Subsidiary to this was the conduct of his whole life. He loved his country partly because it was his own country, but mostly because it was a free country; and he burned with a zeal for its advancement, prosperity and glory, because he saw in such, the advancement, prosperity and glory, of human liberty, human right and human nature. He desired the prosperity of his countrymen partly because they were his countrymen, but chiefly to show to the world that freemen could be prosperous. . . .

When our Federal Constitution was adopted, we owned no territory beyond the limits or ownership of the States, except the territory northwest of the River Ohio, and East of the Mississippi. . . . When, therefore, in 1819, Missouri, having formed a State constitution, without excluding slavery, and with slavery already actually existing within its limits, knocked at the door of the Union for admission, almost the entire representation of the non-slave-holding states, objected. A fearful and angry struggle instantly followed. This alarmed thinking men, more than any previous question, because, unlike all the former, it divided the country by geographical lines. Mr. Clay was in congress, and, perceiving the danger, at once engaged his whole energies to avert it. It began, as I have said, in 1819; and it did not terminate till 1821. . . . All felt that the rejection of Missouri was equivalent to a dissolution of the Union. . . . All deprecated and deplored this, but none saw how to avert it. . . . Coupled with laborious efforts with individual members, and his own over-mastering eloquence upon the floor, he finally secured the admission of the State. Brightly, and captivating as it had previously shown, it was now perceived that his great eloquence, was a mere embellishment, or, at most, but a helping hand to his inventive genius, and his devotion to his country in the day of her extreme peril.

. . . Having been led to allude to domestic slavery so frequently already, I am unwilling to close without referring more particularly to Mr. Clay's views and conduct in regard to it. He ever was, on principle and in feeling, opposed to slavery. The very earliest, and one of the latest public efforts of his life, separated by a period of more than fifty years, were both made in favor of gradual emancipation of the slaves in Kentucky. He did not perceive, that on a question of human right, the negroes were to be excepted from the human race. And yet Mr.

Clay was the owner of slaves. Cast into life where slavery was already widely spread and deeply seated, he did not perceive, as I think no wise man has perceived, how it could be at once eradicated, without producing a greater evil, even to the cause of human liberty itself. His feeling and his judgment, therefore, ever led him to oppose both extremes of opinion on the subject. Those who would shiver into fragments the Union of these States; tear to tatters its now venerated constitution; and even burn the last copy of the Bible, rather than slavery should continue a single hour, together with all their more halting sympathizers, have received, and are receiving their just execration; and the name, and opinions, and influence of Mr. Clay, are fully, and, as I trust, effectually and enduringly, arrayed against them. But I would also, if I could, array his name, opinions, and influence against the opposite extreme—against a few, but an increasing number of men, who, for the sake of perpetuating slavery, are beginning to assail and to ridicule the white-man's charter of freedom—the declaration that "all men are created free and equal."

. . . The American Colonization Society was organized in 1816. Mr. Clay, though not its projector, was one of its earliest members; and he died, as for the many preceding years he had been, its President. It was one of the most cherished objects of his direct care and consideration; and the association of his name with it has probably been its very greatest collateral support. . . . If as the friends of colonization hope, the present and coming generations of our countrymen shall by any means, succeed in freeing our land from the dangerous presence of slavery; and, at the same time, in restoring a captive people to their long-lost fatherland, with bright prospects for the future; and this too, so gradually, that neither races nor individuals shall have suffered by the change, it will indeed be a glorious consummation. And if, to such a consummation, the efforts of Mr. Clay shall have contributed, it will be what he most ardently wished, and none of his labors will have been more valuable to his country and his kind.

But Henry Clay is dead. His long and eventful life is closed. Our country is prosperous and powerful; but could it have been quite all it has been, and is, and is to be, without Henry Clay? Such a man the times have demanded, and such, in the providence of God was given us. But he is gone. Let us strive to deserve, as far as mortals may, the continued care of Divine Providence, trusting that, in future national emergencies, He will not fail to provide us the instruments of safety and security.

SPEECH AT PEORIA, ILLINOIS,
October 16, 1854

The repeal of the Missouri Compromise, and the propriety of its restoration, constitute the subject of what I am about to say. . . . I do not propose to question the patriotism, or to assail the motives of any man, or class of men; but rather to strictly confine myself to the naked merits of the question. I also wish to be no less than National in all the positions I may take; and whenever I take ground which others have thought, or may think, narrow, sectional and dangerous to the Union, I hope to give a reason, which will appear sufficient, at least to some, why I think differently. And, as this subject is no other, than part and parcel of the larger general question of domestic slavery, I wish to MAKE and to KEEP the distinction between the EXISTING institution, and the EXTENSION of it, so broad, and so clear, that no honest man can misunderstand me, and no dishonest one, successfully misrepresent me. . . .

When we established our independence, we did not own, or claim, the country to which this compromise applies. . . . In 1803 we purchased what was then called Louisiana, of France. It included the now states of Louisiana, Arkansas, Missouri, and Iowa; also the territory of Minnesota, and the present bone of contention, Kansas and Nebraska. Slavery already existed among the French at New Orleans; and, to some extent, at St. Louis. In 1812 Louisiana came into the Union as a slave state, without controversy. In 1818 or '19, Missouri showed signs of a wish to come in with slavery. This was resisted by northern members of Congress; and thus began the first great slavery agitation in the nation. This controversy lasted several months, and became very angry and exciting; the House of Representatives voting steadily for the prohibition of slavery in Missouri, and the Senate voting as steadily against it. Threats of breaking up the Union were freely made; and the ablest public men of the day became seriously alarmed. At length a compromise was made, in which, like all compromises, both sides yielded something. It was a law passed on the 6th day of March, 1820, providing that Missouri might come into the Union *with* slavery, but that in all the remaining part of the territory purchased of France, which lies north of 36 degrees and 30 minutes north latitude, slavery should never be permitted. This provision of law, *is the Missouri Compromise*. In excluding slavery North of the line, the same language is employed as in the Ordinance of '87. It directly applied to Iowa, Minnesota, and to the present bone of contention, Kansas and Nebraska. Whether there should or should not, be slavery south of that line, nothing was said in the law; but Arkansas constituted the principal remaining part, south of the line; and it has since been admitted as a slave state without serious controversy. More recently, Iowa, north of the line, came in as a free state without controversy. Still later, Minnesota, north of the line, had a territorial organization without controversy. . . .

Thus originated the Missouri Compromise. . . . Our war with Mexico broke out in 1846. When Congress was about adjourning that session, President Polk asked them to place two millions of dollars under his control, to be used by him in the recess, if found practicable and expedient, in negotiating a treaty of peace with Mexico, and acquiring some part of her territory. A bill was duly got up, for the purpose, and was progressing swimmingly, in the House of Representatives, when a member by the name of David Wilmot, a Democrat from Pennsylvania, moved as an amendment, "Provided that in any territory thus acquired, there shall never be slavery."

This is the origin of the far-famed "Wilmot Proviso." . . . In Dec., 1847, the new congress assembled. I was in the lower House that term. The "Wilmot Proviso" or the principle of it, was constantly coming up in some shape or other, and I think I may venture to say I voted for it at least forty times; during the short term I was there. The Senate, however, held it in check, and it never became law. In the spring of 1848 a treaty of peace was made with Mexico; by which we obtained that portion of her country which now constitutes the territories of New Mexico and Utah, and the now state of California.

By this treaty the Wilmot Proviso was defeated, as so far as it was intended to be, a condition of the acquisition of territory.

. . . In the fall of 1848 the gold mines were discovered in California. This attracted people to it with unprecedented rapidity, so that on, or soon after, the meeting of the new Congress in Dec., 1849, she already had a population of nearly a hundred thousand, had called a convention, formed a state constitution, excluding slavery, and was knocking for admission into the Union. The Proviso men, of course were for letting her in, but the Senate, always true to the other side would not consent to her admission. And there California stood, kept *out* of the Union, because she would not let slavery *into* her borders. . . . There were other points of dispute, connected with the general question of slavery, which equally needed adjustment. The South clamored for a more efficient fugitive slave law. The North clamored for the abolition of a peculiar species of slave trade in the District of Columbia, in connection with which, in view from the windows of the capitol, a sort of negro-livery stable, where droves of negroes were collected, temporarily kept, and finally taken to Southern markets, precisely like droves of horses, had been openly maintained for fifty years. Utah and New Mexico needed territorial governments; and whether slavery should or should not be prohibited within them, was another question. . . . These points all needed adjustment; and they were all held up, perhaps wisely to make them help to adjust one another. The Union, now, as in 1820, was thought to be in danger; and devotion to the Union rightfully inclined men to yield somewhat, in points where nothing else could have so inclined them. A compromise was finally effected. The south got their new fugitive-slave law; and the North got California (the far best part of our acquisition from Mexico) as a free State. The south got a provision that New Mexico and Utah, *when admitted as States*, may come in *with* or *without* slavery as they may then choose; and the north got the slave-trade abolished in the District of Columbia. . . . This is the Compromise of 1850.

. . . During this long period of time Nebraska had remained, substantially an uninhabited country, but now emigration to, and settlement within it began to take place. It is about one third as large as the present United States, and its importance so long over-looked, begins to come into view. The restriction of slavery by the Missouri Compromise directly applies to it; in fact, was first made, and has since been maintained, expressly for it. . . . On January 4th, 1854, Judge [Stephen A.] Douglas introduces a new bill to give Nebraska territorial government. He accompanies this bill with a report, in which last, he expressly recommends that the Missouri Compromise shall neither be affirmed nor repealed. Before long the bill is so modified as to make two territories instead of one; calling the southern one Kansas.

. . . About a month after the introduction of the bill, on the Judge's own motion, it is so amended as to declare the Missouri Compromise inoperative and void; and, substantially, that the People who go and settle there may establish slavery, or exclude it, as they may see fit. In this shape the bill passed both branches of Congress, and became a law.[31]

This is the *repeal* of the Missouri Compromise. . . . I think, and shall try to show, that it is wrong; wrong in its direct effect, letting slavery into Kansas and Nebraska—and wrong in its prospective principle, allowing it to spread to every other part of the wide world, where men can be found inclined to take it. This *declared* indifference, but as I must think, covert real zeal for the spread of slavery, I cannot but hate. I hate it because of the monstrous injustice of slavery itself. I hate it because it deprives our republican example of its just influence in the world—enables the enemies of free institutions, with plausibility, to taunt us as hypocrites—causes the real friends of freedom to doubt our sincerity, and especially because it forces so many really good men amongst ourselves into an open war with the very fundamental principles of civil liberty—criticizing the Declaration of Independence, and insisting that there is no right principle of action but *self-interest*.

Before proceeding, let me say I think I have no prejudice against the Southern people. They are just what we would be in their situation. If slavery did not now exist amongst them, they would not introduce it. If it did now exist amongst us, we should not instantly give it up. This I believe of the masses north and south. Doubtless there are individuals, on both sides, who would not hold slaves under any circumstances; and others who would gladly introduce slavery anew, if it were out of existence. We know that some southern men do free their slaves, go north, and become tip-top abolitionists; while some northern ones go south, and become most cruel slave-masters.

When southern people tell us they are no more responsible for the origin of slavery, than we, I acknowledge the fact. When it is said that the institution exists; and that it is very difficult to get rid of it, in any satisfactory way, I can understand and appreciate the saying. I surely will not blame them for not doing what I should not know how to do myself. If all earthly power were given me, I should not know what to do, as to the existing institution. My first impulse would be to free all the slaves, and send them to Liberia, to their own native land. But a moment's reflection would convince me, that whatever of high hope (as I think there is) there may be in this, in the long run, its sudden execution is impossible. If they were all landed there in a day, they would all perish in the next ten days; and there are not surplus shipping and surplus money enough in the world to carry them there in many times ten days. What then? Free them all, and keep them among us as underlings? Is it quite certain that this betters their condition? I think I would not hold one in slavery, at any rate; yet the point is not clear enough for me to denounce people upon. What next? Free them, and make them politically and socially, our equals? My own feelings will not admit of this; and if mine would, we well know that those of the great mass of white people will not. Whether this feeling accords with justice and sound judgment, is not the sole question, if indeed, it is any part of it. A universal feeling, whether well or ill-founded, cannot be safely disregarded. We cannot, then, make them equals. It does seem to me that systems of gradual emancipation might be adopted; but for their tardiness in this, I will not undertake to judge our brethren of the south.

When they remind us of their constitutional rights, I acknowledge them, not grudgingly, but fully, and fairly; and I would give them any legislation for the reclaiming of their fugitives, which should not, in its stringency, be more likely to carry a free man into slavery, than our ordinary criminal laws are to hang an innocent one.

But all this, to my judgment, furnishes no more excuse for permitting slavery to go into our own free territory, than it would for reviving the African slave trade by law. The law which forbids the bringing of slaves *from*

Africa; and that which has so long forbid the taking them *to* Nebraska, can hardly be distinguished on any moral principle; and the repeal of the former could find quite as plausible excuses as that of the latter.

The arguments by which the repeal of the Missouri Compromise is sought to be justified, are these:

First, that the Nebraska country needed a territorial government.

Second, that in various ways, the public had repudiated it, and demanded the repeal; and therefore should not now complain of it.

And lastly, that the repeal establishes a principle, which is intrinsically right.

I will attempt an answer to each of them in its turn.

First, then, if that country was in need of a territorial organization, could it not have had it as well without as with the repeal? Iowa and Minnesota, to both of which the Missouri restriction applied, had, without its repeal, each in succession, territorial organizations. And even, the year before, a bill for Nebraska itself, was within an ace of passing, without the repealing clause; and this in the hands of the same men who are now the champions of repeal. . . . But, say they, because the public had demanded, or rather commanded the repeal, the repeal was to accompany the organization, whenever that should occur. Now I deny that the public ever demanded any such thing—ever repudiated the Missouri Compromise— ever commanded its repeal. I deny it, and call for the proof. . . .

But next it is said that the compromises of '50 and the ratification of them by both political parties, in '52, established a *new principle*, which required the repeal of the Missouri Compromise. This again I deny. I deny it, and demand the proof. I have already stated fully what the compromises of '50 are. The particular part of those measures . . . is the provision in the Utah and New Mexico laws, which permits them when they seek admission into the Union as States, to come in with or without slavery as they shall then see fit. Now I insist this provision was made for Utah and New Mexico, and for no other place whatever. It had no more direct reference to Nebraska than it had to the territories of the moon. . . . If Congress, at that time, intended that all future territories should, when admitted as States, come in with or without slavery, at their own option, why did it not say so? . . . Still further, if they intended to establish the principle that wherever Congress had control, it should be left to the people to do as they thought fit with slavery why did they not authorize the people of the District of Columbia at their adoption to abolish slavery within these limits? I personally know that this has not been left undone, because it was unthought of. It was frequently spoken of by members of Congress and by citizens of Washington six years ago; and I heard no one express a doubt that a system of gradual emancipation, with compensation to owners, would meet the approbation of a large majority of the white people of the District. But without the action of Congress they could say nothing; and Congress said "no."

. . . I now come to consider whether the repeal, with its avowed principle, is intrinsically right. I insist that it is not. . . . Equal justice to the south, it is said, requires us to consent to the extending of slavery to new countries. That is to say, inasmuch as you do not object to my taking my hog to Nebraska, therefore I must not object to you taking your slave. Now, I admit this is perfectly logical, if there is no difference between hogs and negroes. But while you thus require me to deny the humanity of the negro, I wish to ask whether you of the South yourselves, have ever been willing to do as much? . . . In 1820 you joined the North, almost unanimously, in declaring the African slave trade piracy, and in annexing to it the punishment of death. Why did you do this? If you did not feel that it was wrong, why did you join in providing that men should be hung for it? The practice was no more than bringing wild negroes from Africa, to sell to such as would buy them. But you never thought of hanging men for catching and selling wild horses, wild buffaloes or wild bears.

Again, you have amongst you, a sneaking individual, of the class of native tyrants, known as the "SLAVE-DEALER." He watches your necessities, and crawls up to buy your slave, at a speculating price. If you cannot help it, you sell to him; but if you can help it, you drive him from your door. You despise him utterly. You do not recognize him as a friend, or even as an honest man. Your children must not play with his; they may rollick freely with the little negroes, but not with the "slave-dealer's" children. If you are obliged to deal with him, you try to get through the job without so much as touching him. It is common with you to join hands with the men you meet; but with the slave-dealer you avoid the ceremony—instinctively shrinking from the snaky contact. If he grows rich and retires from business, you still remember him, and still keep up the ban of non-intercourse upon him and his family. Now why is this? You do not so treat the man who deals in corn, cattle or tobacco.

And yet again; there are in the United States and territories, including the District of Columbia, 433,643 free blacks. At $500 per head they are worth over two hundred millions of dollars. How comes this vast

amount of property to be running about without owners? We do not see free horses or free cattle running at
large. How is this? All these free blacks are the descendants of slaves, or have been slaves themselves, and they
would be slaves now, but for SOMETHING which has op-
erated on their white owners, inducing them, at vast
pecuniary sacrifices, to liberate them. What is that
SOMETHING? Is there any mistaking it? In all these cases
it is your sense of justice, and human sympathy, continually telling you, that the poor negro has some natural right to himself—that those who deny it, and make
mere merchandise of him, deserve kickings, contempt
and death.

And now, why will you ask us to deny the humanity
of the slave? and estimate him only as the equal of the
hog? Why ask us to do what you will not do yourselves?
Why ask us to do for *nothing*, what two hundred millions of dollars could not induce you to do?

But one great argument in the support of the repeal
of the Missouri Compromise, is still to come. That argument is "the sacred right of self-government." . . . I trust
I understand, and truly estimate the right of self-
government. My faith in the proposition that each man
should do precisely as he pleases with all which is exclusively his own, lies at the foundation of the sense of
justice there is in me. I extend the principles to communities of men, as well as to individuals. I so extend it,
because it is politically wise, as well as naturally just politically wise, in saving us from broils about matters
which do not concern us. Here, or at Washington, I
would not trouble myself with the oyster laws of Virginia, or the cranberry laws of Indiana.

The doctrine of self-government is right—absolutely
and eternally right—but it has no just application, as here

attempted. Or perhaps I should rather say that whether it has such just application depends upon whether a negro is *not* or *is* a man. If he is *not* a man, why in that case, he who *is* a man may, as a matter of self-government, do just as he pleases with him. But if the negro *is* a man, is it not to that extent, a total destruction of self-government, to say that he too shall not govern *himself*? When the white man governs himself that is self-government; but when he governs himself, and also governs *another* man, that is *more* than self-government—that is despotism. If the negro is a *man*, why then my ancient faith teaches me that "all men are created equal"; and that there can be no moral right in connection with one man's making a slave of another. . . . No man is good enough to govern another man, without that other's consent. I say this is the leading principle—the sheet anchor of American republicanism. Our Declaration of Independence says:

> We hold these truths to be self-evident: that all
> men are created equal; that they are endowed by
> their Creator with certain inalienable rights; that
> among these are life, liberty and the pursuit of
> happiness. That to secure these rights, govern-
> ments are instituted among men, DERIVING
> THEIR JUST POWERS FROM THE CONSENT OF THE
> GOVERNED.

I have quoted so much at this time merely to show that according to our ancient faith, the just powers of governments are derived from the consent of the governed. Now the relation of masters and slaves is, PRO TANTO,[32] a total violation of this principle. The master not only governs the slave without his consent; but he governs him by a set of rules altogether different from those which he prescribes for himself. Allow ALL the governed an equal voice in the government, and that, and that only is self-government.

Let it not be said I am contending for the establishment of political and social equality between the whites and blacks. I have already said the contrary. I am not now combating the argument of NECESSITY, arising from the fact that the blacks are already amongst us; but I am combating what is set up as MORAL argument for allowing them to be taken where they have never yet been—arguing against the EXTENSION of a bad thing, which where it already exists, we must of necessity, manage as we best can.

. . . But you say this question should be left to the people of Nebraska, because they are more particularly interested. If this be the rule, you must leave it to each individual to say for himself whether he will have slaves. . . . But if it is a sacred right for the people of Nebraska to take and hold slaves there, it is equally their sacred right to buy them where they can buy them cheapest; and that undoubtedly will be on the coast of Africa; provided you will consent to not hang them for going there to buy them. You must remove this restriction too, from the sacred right of self-government. I am aware you say that taking slaves from the States to Nebraska, does not make slaves of freemen; but the African slave-trader can say just as much. He does not catch free negroes and bring them here. He finds them already slaves in the hands of their black captors, and he honestly buys them at the rate of about a red cotton handkerchief a head. This is very cheap, and it is a great abridgement of the sacred right of self-government to hang men for engaging in this profitable trade!

. . . Whether slavery shall go into Nebraska, or other new territories, is not a matter of exclusive concern to the people who may go there. The whole nation is interested that the best use shall be made of these territories. We want them for the homes of free white people. This they cannot be, to any considerable extent, if slavery shall be planted within them. Slave States are places for poor white people to remove FROM; not to remove TO. New free States are the places for poor people to go to and better their condition. For this use, the nation needs these territories. . . . I do not, for that cause, or any other cause, propose to destroy, or alter, or disregard the constitution. I stand to it, fairly, fully, and firmly. But when I am told I must leave it altogether to OTHER PEOPLE to say whether new partners are to be bred up and brought into the firm, on the same degrading terms against me, I respectfully demur. . . . I insist, that if there is ANY THING which it is the duty of the WHOLE PEOPLE to never entrust to any hands but their own, that thing is the preservation and perpetuity, of their own liberties, and institutions. And if they shall think, as I do, that the extension of slavery endangers them, more than any, or all other causes, how recreant to themselves, if they submit the question, and with it, the fate of their country, to a mere handful of men, bent only on temporary self-interest. If this question of slavery extension were an insignificant one—one having no power to do harm—it might be shuffled aside in this way. But being, as it is, the great Behemoth of danger, shall the strong gripe of the nation be loosened upon him, to entrust him to the hands of such feeble keepers?

I have done with this mighty argument, of self-government. Go, sacred thing! Go in peace.

But Nebraska is urged as a great Union-saving measure. Well I too, go for saving the Union. Much as I hate slavery, I would consent to the extension of it rather than see the Union dissolved, just as I would consent to any GREAT evil, to avoid a GREATER one. But when I go to Union saving, I must believe, at least, that the means I employ has some adaptation to the end. To my mind, Nebraska has no such adaptation.

"It hath no relish of salvation in it."[33]

It is an aggravation, rather, of the only one thing which ever endangers the Union. When it came upon us, all was peace and quiet. The nation was looking to the forming of new bonds of Union; and a long course of peace and prosperity seemed to lie before us. In the whole range of possibility, there scarcely appears to me to have been any thing, out of which the slavery agitation could have been revived, except the very project of repealing the Missouri compromise. Every inch of territory we owned, already had a definite settlement of the slavery question, and by which, all parties were pledged to abide. Indeed, there was no uninhabited country on the continent, which we could acquire; if we except some extreme northern regions, which are wholly out of the question. In this state of case, the genius of Discord himself, could scarcely have invented a way of again setting us by the ears, but by turning back and destroying the peace measures of the past. The councils of that genius seem to have prevailed, the Missouri compromise was repealed; and here we are, in the midst of a new slavery agitation, such, I think, as we have never seen before. . . . And in this aspect, it could not but produce agitation. Slavery is founded in the selfishness of man's nature—opposition to it, in his love of justice. These principles are an eternal antagonism; and when brought into collision so fiercely, as slavery extension brings them, shocks, and throes, and convulsions must ceaselessly follow. Repeal the Missouri compromise—repeal all compromises—repeal the declaration of independence—repeal all past history, you still cannot repeal human nature. It still will be the abundance of man's heart,[34] that slavery extension is wrong; and out of the abundance of his heart, his mouth will continue to speak.

The structure, too, of the Nebraska bill is very peculiar. The people are to decide the question of slavery for themselves; but WHEN they are to decide; or HOW they are to decide; or whether, when the question is once decided, it is to remain so, or is it to be subject to an indefinite succession of new trials, the law does not say. Is it to be decided by the first dozen settlers who arrive there? or is it to await the arrival of a hundred? Is it to be decided by a vote of the people? or a vote of the legislature? or, indeed by a vote of any sort? To these questions, the law gives no answer. . . . Through all this, bowie-knives and six-shooters are seen plainly enough; but never a glimpse of the ballot-box. And, really, what is to be the result of this? . . . Is it not probable that the contest will come to blows, and bloodshed? Could there be a more apt invention to bring about collision and violence, on the slavery question, than this Nebraska project is? . . . And if this fight should begin, is it likely to take a very peaceful, Union-saving turn? Will not the first drop of blood so shed, be the real knell of the Union? . . . And what shall we have in lieu of it? The South flushed with triumph and tempted to excesses; the North, betrayed, as they believe, brooding on wrong and burning for revenge. One side will provoke; the other resent. . . . Already a few in the North, defy all constitutional restraints, resist the execution of the fugitive slave law, and even menace the institution of slavery in the states where it exists. Already a few in the South, claim the constitutional right to take to and hold slaves in the free states—demand the revival of the slave trade; and demand a treaty with Great Britain by which fugitive slaves may be reclaimed from Canada. As yet they are but few on either side. It is a grave question for the lovers of the Union, whether the final destruction of the Missouri Compromise, and with it the spirit of all compromise will or will not embolden and embitter each of these, and fatally increase the numbers of both.

. . . Some men, mostly whigs, who condemn the repeal of the Missouri Compromise, nevertheless hesitate to go for its restoration, lest they be thrown in company with the abolitionist. Will they allow me as an old whig to tell them good humoredly, that I think this is very silly? Stand with anybody that stands RIGHT. Stand with him while he is right and PART with him when he goes wrong. Stand WITH the abolitionist in restoring the Missouri Compromise; and stand AGAINST him when he attempts to repeal the fugitive slave law. In the latter case you stand with the Southern disunionist. What of that? You are still right. In both cases you are right. In both cases you oppose the dangerous extremes. In both you stand on middle ground and hold the ship level and steady. In both you are national and nothing less than national. This is good old whig ground. To desert such ground, because of any company, is to be less than a whig—less than a man—less than an American.

I particularly object to the NEW position which the avowed principle of this Nebraska law gives to slavery in the body politic. I object to it because it assumes that there CAN be MORAL RIGHT in the enslaving of one man by another. . . . Let no one be deceived. The spirit of seventy-six and the spirit of Nebraska, are utter antagonisms; and the former is being rapidly displaced by the latter.

Fellow countrymen—Americans south, as well as north, shall we make no effort to arrest this? Already the liberal party throughout the world, express the apprehension "that the one retrograde institution in America, is undermining the principles of progress, and fatally violating the noblest political system the world ever saw."[35] This is not the taunt of enemies, but the warning of friends. Is it quite safe to disregard it—to despise it? Is there no danger to liberty itself, in discarding the earliest practice, and first precept of our ancient faith? In our greedy chase to make profit of the negro, let us beware, lest we "cancel and tear to pieces"[36] even the white man's charter of freedom.

Our republican robe is soiled, and trailed in the dust. Let us repurify it. Let us turn and wash it white, in the spirit, if not the blood, of the Revolution. . . . Let us re-adopt the Declaration of Independence, and with it, the practices, and policy, which harmonize with it. Let North and South—let all Americans—let all lovers of liberty everywhere—join in the great and good work. If we do this, we shall not only have saved the Union; but we shall have so saved it, as to make, and to keep it, forever worthy of the saving. We shall have so saved it, that the succeeding millions of free happy people, the world over, shall rise up, and call us blessed, to the latest generations.[37]

. . . Senator Douglas remarked, in substance, that he had always considered this government was made for the white people and not for the negroes. Why, in point of mere fact, I think so too. But in this remark of the Judge, there is a significance, which I think is the key to the great mistake (if there is any such mistake) which he has made in this Nebraska measure. It shows that the Judge has no very vivid impression that the negro is a human; and consequently has no idea that there can be any moral question in legislating about him. In his view, the question of whether a new country shall be slave or free, is a matter of as utter indifference, as it is whether his neighbor shall plant his farm with tobacco, or stock it with horned cattle. Now, whether this view is right or wrong, it is very certain that the great mass of mankind take a totally different view. They consider slavery a great moral wrong; and their feelings against it, is not evanescent, but eternal. It lies at the very foundation of their sense of justice; and it cannot be trifled with. It is a great and durable element of popular action, and, I think, no statesman can safely disregard it. . . . He should remember that he took us by surprise—astounded us—by this measure. We were thunderstruck and stunned; and we reeled and fell in utter confusion. But we rose each fighting, grasping whatever he could first reach—a scythe—a pitchfork—a chopping axe, or a butcher's cleaver. We struck in the direction of the sound; and we are rapidly closing in upon him. He must not think to divert us from our purpose, by showing us that our drill, our dress, and our weapons, are not entirely perfect and uniform. When the storm shall be past, he shall find us still Americans; no less devoted to the continued Union and prosperity of the country than heretofore.

THE "HOUSE DIVIDED" SPEECH,
SPRINGFIELD, ILLINOIS,
June 16, 1858

M r. President and Gentlemen of the Convention.
If we could first know *where* we are, and *whither* we are tending, we could then better judge *what* to do, and *how* to do it.

We are now far into the *fifth* year, since a policy was initiated, with the *avowed* object, and *confident* promise, of putting an end to slavery agitation.

Under the operation of that policy, that agitation has not only, *not ceased*, but has *constantly augmented*.

In my opinion, it *will* not cease, until a *crisis* shall have been reached, and passed.

"A house divided against itself cannot stand."[38]

I believe this government cannot endure, permanently half *slave* and half *free*.

I do not expect the Union to be *dissolved*—I do not expect the house to *fall*—but I *do* expect it will cease to be divided.

It will become *all* one thing, or *all* the other.

Either the *opponents* of slavery, will arrest the further spread of it, and place it where the public mind shall rest in the belief that it is in course of ultimate extinction; or its *advocates* will push it forward, till it shall become alike lawful in *all* the States, *old* as well as *new*—*North* as well as *South*.

Have we no *tendency* to the latter condition?

Let anyone who doubts, carefully contemplate that now almost complete legal combination-piece of *machinery* so to speak—compounded of the Nebraska doctrine, and the Dred Scott decision. Let him consider not only *what work* the machinery is adapted to do, and *how well* adapted; but also, let him study the *history* of its construction, and trace, if he can, or rather *fail*, if he can, to trace the evidences of design, and concert of action, among its chief bosses, from the beginning.

. . . The new year of 1854 found slavery excluded from more than half the States by State Constitutions, and from most of the national territory by Congressional prohibition.

Four days later, commenced the struggle, which ended in repealing that Congressional prohibition.[39]

This opened all the national territory to slavery; and was the first point gained. . . .

This necessity had not been overlooked; but had been provided for, as well as might be, in the notable argument of "*squatter sovereignty*," otherwise called "*sacred right of self-government*," which latter phrase, though expressive of the only rightful basis of any government, was so perverted in this attempted use of it as to amount to just this: That if any *one* man, choose to enslave another, no *third* man shall be allowed to object.

That argument was incorporated into the Nebraska bill itself, in the language which follows: "*It being the true intent and meaning of this act not to legislate slavery into any Territory or state, nor exclude it therefrom; but to leave the people thereof perfectly free to form and regulate their domestic institutions in their own way, subject only to the Constitution of the United States.*"

Then opened the roar of loose declamation in favor of "Squatter Sovereignty," and "Sacred right of self-government."

"But," said opposition members, "let us be more *specific*—let us *amend* the bill so as to expressly declare that the people of the territory *may* exclude slavery."

"Not we," said the friends of the measure; and down they voted the amendment.

While the Nebraska bill was passing through Congress, a *law case*, involving the question of a negro's freedom, by reason of his owner having voluntarily taken him first into a free state and then a territory covered by the congressional prohibition, and held him as a slave, for a long time in each, was passing through the U.S. Circuit Court for the District of Missouri; and both Nebraska bill and law suit were brought to a decision in the same month of May, 1854. The negro's name was Dred Scott, which name now designates the decision finally made in the case.

Before the *then* next Presidential election, the law case came *to*, and was argued *in* the Supreme Court of the United States; but the *decision* of it was deferred until *after* the election. Still, *before* the election, Senator [Lyman] Trumbull, on the floor of the Senate, requests the leading advocate of the Nebraska bill to state *his opinion* whether the people of a territory can constitutionally exclude slavery from their limits; and the latter answers, "That is a question for the Supreme Court."

The election came. Mr. Buchanan was elected, and the *endorsement*, such as it was, secured. That was the *second* point gained. The endorsement, however, fell short of a clear popular majority by nearly four hundred thousand votes, and so, perhaps, was not overwhelmingly reliable and satisfactory.

The *outgoing* President, in his last annual message, as impressively as possible *echoed back* upon the people the *weight* and *authority* of the endorsement.[40]

The Supreme Court met again; *did not* announce their decision, but ordered a re-argument.

The Presidential inauguration came, and still no decision of the court; but the *incoming* President,[41] in his inaugural address, fervently exhorted the people to abide by the forthcoming decision, *whatever it might be.*

Then, in a few days, came the decision.[42]

The reputed author of the Nebraska bill finds an early occasion to make a speech at this capitol indorsing the *Dred Scott* decision, and vehemently denouncing all opposition to it.

. . . At length a squabble springs up between the President and the author of the Nebraska bill, on the *mere* question of *fact*, whether the Lecompton constitution[43] was or was not, in any just sense, made by the people of Kansas; and in that squabble the latter declares that all he wants is a fair vote for the people, and that he *cares* not whether slavery be voted *down* or voted *up*.[44] I do not understand his declaration that he cares not whether slavery be voted down or voted up, to be intended by him other than as an *apt definition* of the *policy* he would impress upon the public mind—the *principle* for which he declares he has suffered much, and is ready to suffer to the end.

And well may he cling to that principle. If he has any parental feeling, well may he cling to it. That principle, is the only *shred* left of his original Nebraska doctrine. Under the Dred Scott decision, "squatter sovereignty" squatted out of existence, tumbled down like temporary scaffolding. . . . His late *joint* struggle with the Republicans, against the Lecompton Constitution, involves nothing of the original Nebraska doctrine. That struggle was made on a point, the right of a people to make their own constitution, upon which he and the Republicans have never differed.

The several points of the *Dred Scott* decision, in connection with Senator Douglas' "care not" policy, constitute the piece of machinery, in its *present* state of advancement. This was the third point gained.

The *working* points of that machinery are:

First, that no negro slave, imported as such from Africa, and no descendant of such slave can ever be a *citizen* of any State, in the sense of that term as used in the Constitution of the United States.[45] This point is made in order to deprive the negro, in every possible event, of the benefit of this provision of the United States Constitution, which declares that—"The citizens of each State shall be entitled to all privileges and immunities of citizens in the several States."

Secondly, that "subject to the Constitution of the United States," neither *Congress* nor a *Territorial Legislature* can exclude slavery from any United States territory. This point is made in order that individual men may *fill up* the territories with slaves, without danger of losing them as property, and thus to enhance the chances of *permanency* to the institution through all the future.

Thirdly, that whether the holding a negro in actual slavery in a free State, makes him free, as against the holder, the United States courts will not decide, but will leave to be decided by the courts of any slave State the negro may be forced into by the master. This point is made, not to be pressed *immediately*; but, if acquiesced in for a while, and apparently *indorsed* by the people at an election, *then* to sustain the logical conclusion that what Dred Scott's master might lawfully do with Dred Scott, in the free State of Illinois, every other master may lawfully do with any other *one*, or one *thousand* slaves, in Illinois, or in any other free State.

Auxiliary to all this, and working hand in hand with it, the Nebraska doctrine, or what is left of it, is to *educate* and *mold* public opinion, at least *Northern* public opinion, to not *care* whether slavery is voted *down* or voted *up*.

This shows exactly where we now *are*; and *partially* also, whither we are tending.

It will throw additional light on the latter, to go back, and run the mind over the string of historical facts already stated. Several things will *now* appear less *dark* and *mysterious* than they did *when* they were transpiring. . . . These things *look* like the cautious *patting* and *petting* a spirited horse, preparatory to mounting him, when it is dreaded that he may give the rider a fall.

. . . We cannot absolutely *know* that all these exact adaptations are the result of preconcert. But when we see a lot of framed timbers, different portions of which we know have been gotten out at different times and places and by different workmen—Stephen, Franklin, Roger and James,[46] for instance—and when we see these timbers joined together, and see they exactly make the frame of a house or a mill, all the tenons and mortices exactly fitting, and all the lengths and proportions of the different pieces exactly adapted to their respective places, and not a piece too many or too few—not omitting even scaffolding—or, if a single piece be lacking, we can see the place in the frame exactly fitted and prepared to yet bring such piece in—in *such* a case, we find it impossible to not *believe* that Stephen and Franklin and Roger and James all understood one another from the beginning, and all worked upon a common *plan* or *draft* drawn up before the first lick was struck. . . . Put *that* and *that* together, and we have another nice little niche, which we may, ere long, see filled with another Supreme Court decision, declaring that the Constitution of the United States does not permit a *state* to exclude slavery from its limits. . . .

Such a decision is all that slavery now lacks of being alike lawful in all the States.

Welcome or unwelcome, such decision *is* probably coming, and will soon be upon us, unless the power of the present political dynasty shall be met and overthrown.

We shall *lie down* pleasantly dreaming that the people of *Missouri* are on the verge of making their State *free*; and we shall *awake* to the *reality*, instead, that the *Supreme* Court has made *Illinois* a *slave* State.

To meet and overthrow the power of that dynasty, is the work now before all those who would prevent that consummation.

That is *what* we have to do.

But *how* can we best do it?

There are those who denounce us *openly* to their *own* friends, and yet whisper *us softly*, that *Senator* [Stephen A.] *Douglas* is the *aptest* instrument there is, with which to effect that object. *They* do *not* tell us, nor has *he* told us, that he *wishes* any such object to be effected. They wish us to *infer* all, from the facts, that he now has a little quarrel with the present head of the dynasty; and that he has regularly voted with us, on a single point, upon which, he and we, have never differed.

They remind us that *he* is a very *great man*, and that the largest of *us* are very small ones. Let this be granted. But "a *living dog* is better than a *dead lion*."[47] Judge Douglas, if not a *dead* lion *for this work*, is at least a *caged* and *toothless* one. How can he oppose the advances of slavery? He don't *care* anything about it. His avowed *mission is impressing* the "public heart" to *care* nothing about it.

. . . Our cause, then, must be entrusted to, and conducted by its own undoubted friends—those whose hands are free, whose hearts are in the work—who *do care* for the result.

Two years ago the Republicans of the nation mustered over thirteen hundred thousand strong.

We did this under the single impulse of resistance to a common danger, with every external circumstance against us.

Of *strange, discordant,* and even, *hostile* elements, we gathered from the four winds, and *formed* and fought the battle through, under the constant hot fire of a disciplined, proud, and pampered enemy.

Did we brave all *then* to *falter* now?—*now*—when that same enemy is *wavering,* dissevered and belligerent?

The result is not doubtful. We shall not fail—if we stand firm, we shall not fail.

Wise councils may *accelerate* or *mistakes delay* it, but, sooner or later the victory is *sure* to come.

SPEECH AT CHICAGO, ILLINOIS,
July 10, 1858

. . . I am not . . . unaware that this Government has endured eighty-two years, half slave and half free. I know that. I am tolerably well acquainted with the history of the country, and I know that it has endured eighty-two years, half slave and half free. I *believe* . . . it has endured because, during all that time, until the introduction of the Nebraska Bill, the public mind did rest, all the time, in the belief that slavery was in course of ultimate extinction. That was what gave us the rest that we had through that period of eighty-two years; at least, so I believe. I have always hated slavery, I think as much as any Abolitionist. I have been an Old Line Whig. I have always hated it, but I have always been quiet about it until this new era of the introduction of the Nebraska Bill began. I always believed that everybody was against it, and that it was in course of ultimate extinction. . . . The adoption of the Constitution and its attendant history led the people to believe so; and that such was the belief of the framers of the Constitution itself. Why did those old men, about the time of the adoption of the Constitution, decree that Slavery should not go into the new Territory, where it had not already gone? Why declare that within twenty years the African Slave Trade, by which slaves are supplied, might be cut off by Congress? Why were all these acts? I might enumerate more of these acts—but enough. What were they but a clear indication that the framers of the Constitution intended and expected the ultimate extinction of that institution. And now, when I say . . . that I think the opponents of slavery will resist the farther spread of it, and place it where the public mind shall rest with the belief that it is in course of ultimate extinction, I only mean to say, that they will place it where the founders of this Government originally placed it.

I have said a hundred times, and I have now no inclination to take it back, that I believe there is no right, and ought to be no inclination in the people of the free States to enter into the slave States, and interfere with the question of slavery at all. I have said that always. Judge Douglas has heard me say it—if not quite a hundred times, at least as good a hundred times; and when it is said that I am in favor of interfering with slavery where it exists, I know it is unwarranted by anything I have ever *intended*, and, as I believe, by anything I have ever *said*. If, by any means, I have ever used language which could fairly be so construed (as, however, I believe I never have), I now correct it.

. . . It so happens that there is a vast portion of the American people that do *not* look upon that matter as being this very little thing. They look upon it as a vast moral evil; they can prove it is such by the writings of those who gave us the blessings of liberty which we enjoy, and that they so looked upon it, and not as an evil merely confining itself to the States where it is situated; and while we agree that, by the Constitution we assented to, in the States where it exists we have no right to interfere with it because it is in the Constitution and we are by both duty and inclination to stick by that Constitution in all its letter and spirit from beginning to end.

. . . I have expressed heretofore, and I now repeat, my opposition to the *Dred Scott* decision, but I should be allowed to state the nature of that opposition. . . . All that I am doing is refusing to obey it as a political rule. If I were in Congress, and a vote should come up on a question whether slavery should be prohibited in a new territory, in spite of that *Dred Scott* decision, I would vote that it should. . . . The sacredness that Judge Douglas throws around this decision, is a degree of sacredness that has never been before thrown around any other decision. I have never heard of such a thing. Why, decisions apparently contrary to that decision, or that good lawyers thought were contrary to that decision, have been made by that very court before. It is the first of its kind; it is an astonisher in legal history. It is a new wonder of the world. It is based upon falsehood in the main as to the facts—allegations of facts upon which it stands are not facts at all in many instances, and no decision made on any question—the first instance of a decision made under so many unfavorable circumstances—thus placed has ever been held by the profession as law, and it has always needed confirmation before the lawyers regarded it as settled law. . . . Do not gentlemen here remember the case of that same Supreme Court, some twenty-five or thirty years ago, deciding that a National Bank was constitutional? . . . General Jackson then said that the Supreme Court had no right to lay down a rule to govern a co-ordinate branch of the government, the members of which had sworn to support the Constitution—that each member had sworn to support that Constitution as he understood it.

. . . We were often—more than once at least—in the course of Judge Douglas' speech last night, reminded that this government was made for white men—that he believed it was made for white men. Well, that is putting it into a shape in which no one wants to deny it, but the Judge then goes into his passion for drawing inferences that are not warranted. I protest, now and forever, against that counterfeit logic which presumes that because I do not want a negro woman for a slave, I do necessarily want her for a wife. My understanding is that I need not have her for either, but as God made us separate, we can leave one another alone and do one another much good thereby. There are white men enough to marry all the white women, and enough black men to marry all the black women, and in God's name let them be so married. The Judge regales us with the terrible enormities that take place by the mixture of races; that the inferior race bears the superior down. Why, Judge, if we do not let them get together in the Territories they won't mix there.

. . . We are now a mighty nation, we are thirty—or about thirty millions of people, and we own and inhabit about one-fifteenth part of the dry land of the whole earth. We run our memory back over the pages of history for about eighty-two years and we discover that we were then a very small people in point of numbers, vastly inferior to what we are now, with a vastly less extent of country,—with vastly less of everything we deem desirable among men,—we look upon the change as exceedingly advantageous to us and to our posterity, and we fix upon something that happened away back, as in some way or other being connected with this rise of prosperity. We find a race of men living in that day whom we claim as our fathers and grandfathers; they were iron men, they fought for the principle that they were contending for; and we understood that by what they then did it has followed that the degree of prosperity that we now enjoy has come to us. But after we have done all this . . . we have besides these men—descended by blood from our ancestors—among us perhaps half our people who are not descendants at all of these men, they are men who have come from Europe—German, Irish, French and Scandinavian—men that have come from Europe themselves, or whose ancestors have come hither and settled here, finding themselves our equals in all things. If they look back through this history to trace their connection with those days by blood, they find they have none, they cannot carry themselves back into that glorious epoch and make themselves feel that they are part of us, but when they look through that old Declaration of Independence they find that those old men say that "We hold these truths to be self-evident, that all men are created equal," and then they feel that that moral sentiment taught in that day evidences their relation to those men, that it is the father of all moral principle in them, and that they have a right to claim it as though they were blood of the blood, and flesh of the flesh of the men who wrote that Declaration, and so they are. That is the electric cord in that Declaration that links the hearts of patriotic and liberty-loving men together, that will link those patriotic hearts as long as the love of freedom exists in the minds of men throughout the world.

. . . Those arguments that are made, that the inferior race are to be treated with as much allowance as they are capable of enjoying; that as much is to be done for them as their condition will allow. What are these arguments? They are the arguments that kings have made for enslaving the people in all ages of the world. You will find that all the arguments in favor of king-craft were of this class; they always bestrode the necks of the people, not that they wanted to do it, but because the people were better off for being ridden. That is their argument, and this argument of the Judge is the same old serpent that says you work and I eat, you toil and I will enjoy the fruits of it. Turn in whatever way you will—whether it come from the mouth of a king, an excuse for enslaving the people of his country, or from the mouth of men of one race as a reason for enslaving the men of another race, it is all the same old serpent, and I hold if that course of argumentation that is made for the purpose of convincing the public mind that we should not care about this, should be granted, it does not stop with the negro. I should like to know if taking this old Declaration of Independence, which declares that all men are equal upon principle and making exceptions to it where will it stop. If one man says it does not mean a negro, why not another say it does not mean some other man?

If that declaration is not the truth, let us get the Statute book, in which we find it and tear it out!

. . . It may be argued that there are certain conditions that make necessities and impose them upon us, and to the extent that a necessity is imposed upon a man he must submit to it. I think that was the condition in which we found ourselves when we established this government. We had slavery among us, we could not get our constitution unless we permitted them to remain in slavery, we could not secure the good we did secure if we grasped for more, and having by necessity submitted to that much, it does not destroy the principle that is the charter of our liberties. Let that charter stand as our standard. My friend has said to me that I am a poor hand to quote Scripture. I will try it again, however. It is said in one of the admonitions of the Lord, "As your Father in Heaven is perfect, be ye also perfect."[48] The Savior, I suppose, did not expect that any human creature could be perfect as the Father in Heaven; but He said, "As your Father in Heaven is perfect, be ye also perfect." He set that up as a standard, and he who did most towards reaching that standard, attained the highest degree of moral perfection. So I say in relation to the principle that all men are created equal, let it be as nearly reached as we can. If we cannot give freedom to every creature, let us do nothing that will impose slavery upon any other creature. Let us then turn this government back into the channel in which the framers of the Constitution originally placed it. . . . Let us discard all this quibbling about this man and the other man—this race and that race and the other race being inferior, and therefore they must be placed in an inferior position—discarding our standard that we have left us. Let us discard all these things, and unite as one people throughout this land, until we shall once more stand up declaring that all men are created equal.

SPEECH AT LEWISTOWN, ILLINOIS,
August 17, 1858

The Declaration of Independence . . . was formed by the representatives of American liberty from thirteen states of the confederacy—twelve of which were slaveholding communities. We need not discuss the way or the reason of their becoming slaveholding communities. It is sufficient for our purpose that *all of them* greatly deplored the evil and that they placed a provision in the Constitution which they supposed would gradually remove the disease by cutting off its source. This was the abolition of the slave trade. So general was conviction—the public determination—to abolish the African slave trade, that the provision which I have referred to as being placed in the Constitution, declared that it should *not* be abolished prior to the year 1808. A constitutional provision was necessary to prevent the people, through Congress, from putting a stop to the traffic immediately at the close of the war. Now, if slavery had been a good thing, would the Fathers of the Republic have taken a step calculated to diminish its beneficent influences among themselves, and snatch the boon wholly from their posterity? These communities, by their representatives in old Independence Hall, said to the whole world of men: "We hold these truths to be self-evident: that all men are created equal; that they are endowed by their Creator with certain unalienable rights; that among these are life, liberty and the pursuit of happiness." This was their majestic interpretation of the economy of the Universe. This was their lofty, and wise, and noble understanding of the justice of the Creator to His creatures. Yes, gentlemen, to *all* his creatures, to the whole great family of man. In their enlightened belief, nothing stamped with the Divine image and likeness was sent into the world to be trodden on, and degraded, and imbruted by its fellows. They grasped not only the whole race of man then living, but they reached forward and seized upon the farthest posterity. They erected a beacon to guide their children and their children's children, and the countless myriads who should inhabit the earth in other ages. Wise statesmen as they were, they knew the tendency of prosperity to breed tyrants, and so they established these great self-evident truths, that when in the distant future some man, some faction, some interest, should set up the doctrine that none but rich men, or none but white men, were entitled to life, liberty and the pursuit of happiness, their posterity might look up again to the Declaration of Independence and take courage to renew the battle which their fathers began— so that truth, and justice, and mercy, and all the humane and Christian virtues might not be extinguished from the land; so that no man would hereafter dare to limit and circumscribe the great principles on which the temple of liberty was being built.

Now, my countrymen . . . if you have been taught doctrines conflicting with the great landmarks of the Declaration of Independence; if you have listened to suggestions which would take away from its grandeur, and mutilate the fair symmetry of its proportions; if you have been inclined to believe that all men are *not* created equal in those inalienable rights enumerated by our chart of liberty, let me entreat you to come back. Return to the fountain whose waters spring close by the blood of the Revolution. Think nothing of me—take no thought for the political fate of any man whomsoever— but come back to the truths that are in the Declaration of Independence. You may do anything with me you choose, if you will but heed these sacred principles. You may not only defeat me for the Senate, but you may take me and put me to death. While pretending no indifference to earthly honors, I *do claim* to be actuated in this contest by something higher than an anxiety for office. I charge you to drop every paltry and insignificant thought for any man's success. It is nothing; I am nothing; Judge Douglas is nothing. *But do not destroy that immortal emblem of Humanity—the Declaration of American Independence.*

FIFTH DEBATE WITH STEPHEN A. DOUGLAS, GALESBURG, ILLINOIS, *October 7, 1858*

. . . The Judge has alluded to the Declaration of Independence, and insisted that negroes are not included in that Declaration; and that it is a slander upon the framers of that instrument, to suppose that negroes were meant therein; and he asks you: Is it possible to believe that Mr. Jefferson, who penned the immortal paper, could have supposed himself applying the language of that instrument to the negro race, and yet held a portion of that race in slavery? Would he not at once have freed them? I only have to remark upon this part of the Judge's speech (and that, too, very briefly, for I shall not detain myself, or you, upon that point for any great length of time), that I believe the entire records of the world, from the date of the Declaration of Independence up to within three years ago, may be searched in vain for one single affirmation, from one single man, that the negro was not included in the Declaration of Independence. I think I may defy Judge Douglas to show that he ever said so, that Washington ever said so, that any President ever said so, that any member of Congress ever said so, or that any living man upon the whole earth ever said so, until the necessities of the present policy of the Democratic party, in regard to slavery, had to invent that affirmation.

. . . I have all the while maintained, that in so far as it should be insisted that there was an equality between the white and black races that should produce a perfect social and political equality, it was an impossibility. This you have seen in my printed speeches, and with it I have said, that in their right to "life, liberty and the pursuit of happiness," as proclaimed in that old Declaration, the inferior races are our equals. And these declarations I have constantly made in reference to the abstract moral question, to contemplate and consider when we are legislating about any new country which is not already cursed with the actual presence of the evil—slavery. I have never manifested any impatience with the necessities that spring from the actual presence of black people amongst us, and the actual existence of slavery amongst us where it does already exist; but I have insisted that, in legislating for new countries, where it does not exist, there is no just rule other than that of moral and abstract right! With reference to those new countries, those maxims as to the right of a people to "life, liberty and the pursuit of happiness," were the just rules to be constantly referred to.

. . . I have always maintained, so far as I was able, that there was nothing of the principle of the Nebraska bill in the compromise of 1850 at all—nothing whatever. Where can you find the principle of the Nebraska bill in that compromise? If anywhere, in the two pieces of the compromise organizing the Territories of New Mexico and Utah. . . . I maintain that the organization of Utah and New Mexico *did not* establish a general principle at all. It had no feature of establishing a general principle. . . . They did not lay down what was proposed as a regular policy for the Territories; only an agreement in this particular case to do in that way, because other things were done that were to be a compensation for it. . . . My own opinion is, that a thorough investigation will show most plainly that the New Mexico and Utah bills were part of a system of compromise, and not designed as patterns for future territorial legislation; and that this Nebraska bill did not follow them as a pattern at all.

. . . I suppose that the real difference between Judge Douglas and his friends, and the Republicans on the contrary, is that the Judge is not in favor of making any difference between Slavery and Liberty—that he is in favor of eradicating, of pressing out of view, the questions of preference in this country for Free over Slave institutions; and consequently every sentiment he utters discards the idea that there is any wrong in Slavery. Everything that emanates from him or his coadjutors in their course of policy, carefully excludes the thought that there is anything wrong in Slavery. All their arguments, if you will consider them, will be seen to exclude the thought that there is anything whatever wrong in Slavery. If you will take the Judge's speeches, and select the short and pointed sentences expressed by him—as his declaration that he "don't care whether Slavery is voted up or down"—you will see at once that this is perfectly logical, if you do not admit that Slavery is wrong. . . . He insists that, upon the score of equality, the owners of slaves and owners of property—of horses and every other sort of property—should be alike and hold them alike in a new Territory. That is perfectly logical, if the two species of property are alike and are equally founded in right. But if you admit that one of them is wrong, you cannot institute any equality between right and wrong. And from this difference of sentiment—the belief on the part of one that the institution is wrong, and a policy springing from that belief which looks to the arrest of the enlargement of that wrong; and this other sentiment, that it is no wrong, and a policy sprung from that sentiment which will tolerate no idea of preventing that wrong from growing larger, and looks to there never being an end of it through all the existence of things— arises the real difference between Judge Douglas and his friends, on the one hand, and the Republicans on the other. Now, I confess myself as belonging to that class in the country who contemplate slavery as a moral, social and political evil, having due regard for its actual existence amongst us and the difficulties of getting rid of it in any satisfactory way, and to all the constitutional obligations which have been thrown about it; but, nevertheless, desire a policy that looks to the prevention of it as a wrong, and looks hopefully to the time when as a wrong it may come to an end.

. . . While we were at Freeport, in one of these joint discussions, I answered certain interrogatories which

Judge Douglas had propounded to me, and there in turn propounded some to him, which he in a sort of way answered. The third one of these interrogatories I have with me and wish now to make some comments upon it. It was in these words: "If the Supreme Court of the United States shall decide that the States cannot exclude slavery from their limits, are you in favor of acquiescing in, adhering to and following such decision, as a rule of political action?"

To this interrogatory Judge Douglas made no answer in any just sense of the word. He contented himself with sneering at the thought that it was possible for the Supreme Court ever to make such a decision. He sneered at me for propounding the interrogatory. I had not propounded it without some reflection, and I wish now to address to this audience some remarks upon it.

In the second clause of the sixth article, I believe it is of the Constitution of the United States, we find the following language: "This Constitution and the laws of the United States which shall be made in pursuance thereof; and all treaties made or which shall be made under the authority of the United States, shall be the supreme law of the land; and the judges in every State shall be bound thereby anything in the Constitution or laws of any State to the contrary notwithstanding." . . . Now, remembering the provision of the Constitution which I have read, affirming that that instrument is the supreme law of the land; that the Judges of every State shall be bound by it, any law or Constitution of any State to the contrary notwithstanding; that the right of property in a slave is affirmed in that Constitution, is made, formed into and cannot be separated from it without breaking it; durable as the instrument; part of the instrument—what follows as a short and even syllogistic argument from it? I think it follows, and I submit to the consideration of men capable of arguing, whether as I state it in syllogistic form the argument has any fault in it:

Nothing in the Constitution or laws of any State can destroy a right distinctly and expressly affirmed in the Constitution of the United States.

The right of property in a slave is distinctly and expressly affirmed in the Constitution of the United States;

Therefore, nothing in the Constitution or laws of any State can destroy the right of property in a slave.

I believe that no fault can be pointed out in that argument; assuming the truth of the premises, the conclusion, so far as I have capacity at all to understand it, follows inevitably. There is a fault in it as I think, but the fault is not in the reasoning; but the falsehood in fact is a fault of the premises. I believe that the right of property in a slave *is not* distinctly and expressly affirmed in the Constitution, and Judge Douglas thinks it is. I believe that the Supreme Court and the advocates of that decision may search in vain for the place in the Constitution where the right of property in a slave is distinctly and expressly affirmed. I say, therefore, that I think one of the premises is not true in fact. But it is true with Judge Douglas. It is true with the Supreme Court who pronounced it. They are estopped from denying it, and being estopped from denying it, the conclusion follows that the Constitution of the United States being the supreme law, no constitution or law can interfere with it. It being affirmed in the decision that the right of property in a slave is distinctly and expressly affirmed in the Constitution, the conclusion inevitably follows that no State law or constitution can destroy that right. I then say to Judge Douglas and to all others, that I think it will take a better answer than a sneer to show that those who have said that the right of property in a slave is distinctly and expressly affirmed in the Constitution, are not prepared to show that no constitution or law can destroy that right. I say I believe it will take a far better argument than a mere sneer to show to the minds of intelligent men that whoever has so said, is not prepared, whenever public sentiment is so far advanced as to justify it, to say the other.

. . . In this I think I argue fairly (without questioning motives at all) that Judge Douglas is most ingeniously and powerfully preparing the public mind to take that decision when it comes; and not only so, but he is doing it in various other ways. In these general maxims about liberty—in his assertions that he "don't care whether Slavery is voted up or voted down"; that "whoever wants Slavery has a right to have it"; that "upon principles of equality it should be allowed to go everywhere"; that "there is no inconsistency between free and slave institutions." In this he is also preparing (whether purposely or not), the way for making the institution of Slavery national! I repeat again, for I wish no misunderstanding, that I do not charge that he means it so; but I call upon your minds to inquire, if you were going to get the best instrument you could, and then set it to work in the most ingenious way, to prepare the public mind for this movement, operating in the free States, where there is now an abhorrence of the institution of Slavery, could you find an instrument so capable of doing it as Judge Douglas? or one employed in so apt a way to do it? . . . Whoever like him teaches that the negro has no share, humble though it may be, in the Declaration of Independence, is going back to the era of our liberty and independence, and, so far as in him lies, muzzling the cannon that thunders its annual joyous return; that he is blowing out the moral lights around us, when he contends that whoever wants slaves has a right to hold them; that he is penetrating, so far as lies in his power, the human soul, and eradicating the light of reason and the love of liberty, when he is in every possible way preparing the public mind, by his vast influence, for making the institution of slavery perpetual and national.

. . . If Judge Douglas' policy upon this question succeeds, and gets fairly settled down, until all opposition is crushed out, the next thing will be a grab for the territory of poor Mexico, an invasion of the rich lands of South America, then the adjoining islands will follow, each one of which promises additional slave fields.

. . . And now it only remains for me to say that I think it is a very grave question for the people of this Union to consider whether, in view of the fact that this Slavery question has been the only one that has ever endangered our republican institutions—the only one that has ever threatened or menaced a dissolution of the Union—that has ever disturbed us in such a way as to make us fear for the perpetuity of our liberty—in view of these facts, I think it is an exceedingly interesting and important question for this people to consider, whether we shall engage in the policy of acquiring additional territory, discarding altogether from our consideration, while obtaining new territory, the question how it may affect us in regard to this the only endangering element to our liberties and national greatness.

SIXTH DEBATE WITH
STEPHEN A. DOUGLAS,
QUINCY, ILLINOIS,
October 13, 1858

. . . I was aware, when it was first agreed that Judge Douglas and I were to have these seven joint discussions, that they were the successive acts of a drama—perhaps I should say, to be enacted not merely in the face of audiences like this, but in the face of the nation, and to some extent, by my relation to him, and not from anything in myself, in the face of the world; and I am anxious that they should be conducted with dignity and in the good temper which would be befitting the vast audience before which it was conducted. But when Judge Douglas got home from Washington and made his first speech in Chicago, the evening afterwards I made some sort of a reply to it. His second speech was made at Bloomington, in which, he commented upon my speech at Chicago, and said that I had used language ingeniously contrived to conceal my intentions, or words to that effect. Now, I understand that this is an imputation upon my veracity and my candor. I do not know what the Judge understood by it; but in our first discussion at Ottawa, he led off by charging a bargain, somewhat corrupt in its character, upon [Senator Lyman] Trumbull and myself—that we had entered into a bargain, one of the terms of which was that Trumbull was to abolitionize the old Democratic party, and I (Lincoln) was to abolitionize the old Whig party—I pretending to be as good an Old Line Whig as ever. Judge Douglas may not understand that he implicated my truthfulness and my honor, when he said I was doing one thing and pretending another; and I misunderstood him if he thought he was treating me in a dignified way, as a man of honor and truth, as he now claims he was disposed to treat me. Even after that time, at Galesburg, when he brings forward an extract from a speech made at Chicago, and an extract from a speech made at Charleston, to prove that I was trying to play a double part—that I was trying to cheat the public, and get votes upon one set of principles at one place and upon another set of principles at another place—I do not understand but what he impeaches my honor, my veracity and my candor, and because *he* does this, I do not understand that I am bound, if I see a truthful ground for it, to keep my hands off of him. As soon as I learned that Judge Douglas was disposed to treat me in this way, I signified in one of my speeches that I should be driven to draw upon whatever of humble re-sources I might have—to adopt a new course with him. I was not entirely sure that I should be able to hold my own with him, but I at least had the purpose made to do as well as I could upon him; and now I say that I will not be the first to cry "hold."[49] I think it originated with the Judge, and when he quits, I probably will. But I shall not ask any favors at all. He asks me, or he asks the audience, if I wish to push this matter to the point of personal difficulty. I tell him, no. He did not make a mistake, in one of his early speeches, when he called me an "amiable" man, though perhaps he did when he called me an "intelligent" man. It really hurts me very much to suppose that I have wronged anybody on earth. I again tell him, no! I very much prefer, when this canvass shall be over, however it may result, that we at least part without any bitter recollections of personal difficulties.

. . . We have in this nation this element of domestic slavery. It is a matter of absolute certainty that it is a disturbing element. It is the opinion of all the great men who have expressed an opinion upon it, that it is a dangerous element. We keep up a controversy in regard to it. That controversy necessarily springs from difference of opinion, and if we can learn exactly—can reduce to the lowest elements—what that difference of opinion is, we perhaps shall be better prepared for discussing the different systems of policy that we would propose in regard to that disturbing element. I suggest that the difference of opinion, reduced to its lowest terms, is no other than the difference between the men who think slavery a wrong and those who do not think it wrong. The Republican party think it wrong—we think it is a moral, a social and a political wrong. We think it is a wrong not confining itself merely to the persons or the States where it exists, but that it is a wrong in its tendency, to say the least, that extends itself to the existence of the whole nation. Because we think it wrong, we propose a course of policy that shall deal with it as a wrong. We deal with it as with any other wrong, in so far as we can prevent its growing any larger, and so deal with it that in the run of time there may be some promise of an end to it. We have a due regard to the actual presence of it amongst us and the difficulties of getting rid of it in any satisfactory way, and all the constitutional obligations thrown about it. I suppose that in reference both to its actual existence in the nation, and to our constitutional obligations, we have no right at all to disturb it in the States where it exists, and we profess that we have no more inclination to disturb it than we have the right to do it. We go further than that; we don't propose to disturb it where, in one instance, we think the Constitution would permit us. We think the Constitution would permit us to disturb it in the District of Columbia. Still we do not propose to do that, unless it should be in terms which I don't suppose the nation is very likely soon to agree to—the terms of making the emancipation gradual and compensating the unwilling owners. Where we suppose we have the constitutional right, we restrain ourselves in reference to the actual existence of the institution and the difficulties thrown about it. We also oppose it as an evil so far as it seeks to spread itself. We insist on the policy that shall restrict it to its present limits. We don't suppose that in doing this we violate anything due to the actual presence of the institution, or anything due to the constitutional guarantees thrown around it.

We oppose the Dred Scott decision in a certain way, upon which I ought perhaps to address you a few words. We do not propose that when Dred Scott has been decided to be a slave by the court, we, as a mob, will decide him to be free. We do not propose that, when any other one, or one thousand, shall be decided by that court to be slaves, we will in any violent way disturb the rights of property thus settled; but we nevertheless do oppose that decision as a political rule which shall be binding on the voter, to vote for nobody who thinks it wrong, which shall be binding on the members of Congress or the President to favor no measure that does not actually concur with the principles of that decision. We do not propose to be bound by it as a political rule in that way, because we think it lays the foundation not merely of enlarging and spreading out what we consider an evil, but it lays the foundation for spreading that evil into the States themselves. We propose so resisting it as to have it reversed if we can, and a new judicial rule established upon this subject.

I will add this, that if there be any man who does not

believe that slavery is wrong in the three aspects which I have mentioned, or in any one of them, that man is misplaced, and ought to leave us. While, on the other hand, if there be any man in the Republican party who is impatient over the necessity springing from its actual presence, and is impatient of the constitutional guarantees thrown around it, and would act in disregard of these, he too is misplaced standing with us. He will find his place somewhere else; for we have a due regard, so far as we are capable of understanding them, for all these things. This, gentlemen, as well as I can give it, is a plain statement of our principles in all their enormity.

I will say now that there is a sentiment in the country contrary to me—a sentiment which holds that slavery is not wrong, and therefore it goes for policy that does not propose dealing with it as a wrong. That policy is the Democratic policy, and that sentiment is the Democratic sentiment. If there be a doubt in the mind of any one of this vast audience that this is really the central idea of the Democratic party, in relation to this subject, I ask him to bear with me while I state a few things tending, as I think, to prove that proposition. In the first place, the leading man—I think I may do my friend Judge Douglas the honor of calling him such—advocating the present Democratic policy, never himself says it is wrong. He has the high distinction, so far as I know, of never having said slavery is either right or wrong. Almost everybody else says one or the other, but the Judge never does. If there be a man in the Democratic party who thinks it is wrong, and yet clings to that party, I suggest to him in the first place that his leader don't talk as he does, for he never says that it is wrong. In the second place, I suggest to him that if he will examine the policy proposed to be carried forward, he will find that he carefully excludes the idea that there is anything wrong in it. If you will examine the arguments that are made on it, you will find that everyone carefully excludes the idea that there is anything wrong in slavery. Perhaps that Democrat who says he is as much opposed to slavery as I am, will tell me that I am wrong about this. I wish him to examine his own course in regard to this matter a moment, and then see if his opinion will not be changed a little. You say it is wrong; but don't you constantly object to anybody else saying so? Do you not constantly argue that this is not the right place to oppose it? You say it must not be opposed in the free States, because slavery is not here; it must not be opposed in the slave States, because it is there; it must not be opposed in politics, because that will make a fuss; it must not be opposed in the pulpit, because it is not religion. Then where is the place to oppose it? There is no suitable place to oppose it. There is no place in the country to oppose this evil overspreading the continent, which you say yourself is coming. . . . So I say again that in regard to the arguments that are made, when Judge Douglas says he "don't care whether slavery is voted up or voted down," whether he means that as an individual expression of sentiment, or only as a sort of statement of his views on national policy, it is alike true to say that he can thus argue logically if he don't see anything wrong in it; but he cannot say so logically if he admits that slavery is wrong. He cannot say that he would as soon see a wrong voted up as voted down. When Judge Douglas says that whoever, or whatever community, wants slaves, they have a right to have them, he is perfectly logical if there is nothing wrong in the institution; but if you admit that it is wrong, he cannot logically say that anybody has a right to do wrong. When he says that slave property and horse and hog property are alike to be allowed to go into the Territories, upon the principles of equality, he is reasoning truly, if there is no difference between them as property; but if the one is property, held rightfully, and the other is wrong, then there is no equality between the right and wrong; so that, turn it in any-way you can, in all the arguments sustaining the Democratic policy, and in that policy itself, there is a careful, studied exclusion of the idea that there is anything wrong in slavery. Let us understand this. I am not, just here, trying to prove that we are right and they are wrong. I have been stating where we and they stand, and trying to show what is the real difference between us; and I now say that whenever we can get the question distinctly stated—can get all these men who believe that slavery is in some of these respects wrong, to stand and act with us in treating it as a wrong—then, and not till then, I think we will in some way come to an end of this slavery agitation.

SEVENTH DEBATE WITH STEPHEN A. DOUGLAS, ALTON, ILLINOIS,
October 15, 1858

. . . It is not true that our fathers, as Judge Douglas assumes, made this government part slave and part free. Understand the sense in which he puts it. He assumes that slavery is a rightful thing within itself—was introduced by the framers of the Constitution. The exact truth is, that they found the institution existing among us, and they left it as they found it. But in making the government they left this institution with many clear marks of disapprobation upon it. They found slavery among them and they left it among them because of the difficulty—the absolute impossibility of its immediate removal. And when Judge Douglas asks me why we cannot let it remain part slave and part free as the fathers of the government made, he asks a question based upon an assumption which is itself a falsehood; and I turn upon him and ask him the question, when the policy that the fathers of the government had adopted in relation to this element among us was the best policy in the world—the only wise policy—the only policy that we can ever safely continue upon—that will ever give us peace unless this dangerous element masters us all and becomes a national institution—*I turn upon him and ask him why he could not let it alone?* I turn and ask him why he was driven to the necessity of introducing a *new* policy in regard to it? . . . I ask you when he infers that I am in favor of setting the free and slave States at war, when the institution was placed in that attitude by those who made the constitution, *did they make any war?* If we had no war out of it when thus placed, wherein is the ground of belief that we shall have war out of it if we return to that policy? Have we had any peace upon this matter springing from any other basis? I maintain that we have not. I have proposed nothing more than a return to the policy of the fathers.

. . . How many times have we had danger from this question? Go back to the day of the Missouri Compromise. Go back to the Nullification question, at the bottom of which lay this same slavery question. Go back to the time of the Annexation of Texas. Go back to the troubles that led to the Compromise of 1850. You will find that every time, with the single exception of the Nullification question, they sprung from an endeavor to spread this institution. There never was a party in the history of this country, and there probably never will be of sufficient strength to disturb the general peace of the country. Parties themselves may be divided and quarrel on minor questions, yet it extends not beyond the parties themselves. But does *not* this question make a disturbance outside of political circles? Does it not enter into the churches and rend them asunder? What divided the great Methodist Church into two parts, North and South? What has raised this constant disturbance in every Presbyterian General Assembly that meets? What disturbed the Unitarian Church in this very city two years ago? What has jarred and shaken the great American Tract Society recently, not yet splitting it, but sure to divide it in the end? Is it not this same mighty, deep seated power that somehow operates on the minds of men, exciting and stirring them up in every avenue of society—in politics, in religion, in literature, in morals, in all the manifold relations of life? Is this the work of politicians? Is that irresistible power which for fifty years has shaken the government and agitated the people to be stilled and subdued by pretending that it is an exceedingly simple thing, and we ought not to talk about it?

. . . We have no power as citizens of the free States or in our federal capacity as members of the Federal Union through the general government, to disturb slavery in the States where it exists. We profess constantly that we have no more inclination than belief in the power of the Government to disturb it; yet we are driven constantly to defend ourselves from the assumption that we are warring upon the rights of the *States*. What I insist upon is, that the new Territories shall be kept free from it while in the Territorial condition. Judge Douglas assumes that we have no interest in them—that we have no right whatever to interfere. I think we have some interest. I think that as white men we have. Do we not wish for an outlet for our surplus population, if I may so express myself? Do we not feel an interest in getting to that outlet with such institutions as we would like to have prevail there? If *you* go to the Territory opposed to slavery and another man comes upon the same ground with his slave, upon the assumption that the things are equal, it turns out that he has the equal right all his way and you have no part of it your way. If he goes in and makes it a slave Territory, and by consequence a slave State, is it not time that those who desire to have it a free State were on equal ground?

. . . Now irrespective of the moral aspect of this question as to whether there is a right or wrong in enslaving a negro, I am still in favor of our new Territories being in such a condition that white men may find a home—may find some spot where they can better their condition—where they can settle upon new soil and better their condition in life. I am in favor of this not merely (I must say it here as I have elsewhere), for our own people who are born amongst us, but as an outlet for *free white people everywhere*, the world over—in which Hans and Baptiste and Patrick, and all other men from all the world, may find new homes and better their conditions in life.

I have stated upon former occasions, and I may as well state again, what I understand to be the real issue in this controversy between Judge Douglas and myself. On the point of my wanting to make war between the free and the slave States, there has been no issue between us. So, too, when he assumes that I am in favor of introducing a perfect social and political equality between the white and black races. These are false issues, upon which Judge Douglas has tried to force the controversy. There is no foundation in truth for the charge that I maintain either of these propositions. The real issue in this controversy—the one pressing upon every mind—is the sentiment on the part of one class that looks upon the institution of slavery *as a wrong*, and of another class that *does not* look upon it as a wrong. The sentiment that contemplates the institution of slavery in this country as a wrong is the sentiment of the Republican party. It is the sentiment around which all their actions—all their arguments circle—from which all their propositions radiate. They look upon it as being a moral, social and political wrong; and while they contemplate it as such, they nevertheless have due regard for its actual existence among us, and the difficulties of getting rid of it in any satisfactory way and to all the constitutional obligations thrown about it. Yet having a due regard for these, they desire a policy in regard to it that looks to its not creating any more danger. They insist that it should as far as may be, *be treated* as a wrong, and one of the methods of treating it as a wrong is to *make provision that it shall grow no larger*. They also desire a policy that looks to a peaceful end of slavery at some time, as being wrong. . . .

That is the real issue. That is the issue that will continue in this country when these poor tongues of Judge Douglas and myself shall be silent. It is the eternal struggle between these two principles—right and wrong—throughout the world. They are the two principles that have stood face to face from the beginning of time; and will ever continue to struggle. The one is the common right of humanity and the other the divine right of kings. It is the same principle in whatever shape it develops itself. It is the same spirit that says, "You work and toil and earn bread, and I'll eat it." No matter in what shape it comes, whether from the mouth of a king who seeks to bestride the people of his own nation and live by the fruit of their labor, or from one race of men as an apology for enslaving another race, it is the same tyrannical principle.

ADDRESS BEFORE THE WISCONSIN STATE AGRICULTURAL SOCIETY, MILWAUKEE, WISCONSIN,
September 30, 1859

Members of the Agricultural Society and Citizens of Wisconsin:

Agricultural Fairs are becoming an institution of the country; they are useful in more ways than one; they bring us together, and thereby make us better acquainted, and better friends than we otherwise would be. . . . But the chief use of agricultural fairs is to aid in improving the great calling of *agriculture*, in all its departments, and minute divisions—to make mutual exchange of agricultural discovery, information, and knowledge; so that, at the end, *all* may know everything, which may have been known to but *one*, or to but a *few*, at the beginning—to bring together especially all which is supposed to not be generally known, because of recent discovery, or invention.

And not only to bring together, and to impart all

which has been *accidentally* discovered or invented upon ordinary motive; but, by exciting emulation, for premiums, and for the pride and honor of success—of triumph, in some sort—to stimulate that discovery and invention into extraordinary activity. In this, these Fairs are kindred to the patent clause in the Constitution of the United States; and to the department, and practical system, based upon that clause.

. . . The world is agreed that *labor* is the source from which human wants are mainly supplied. There is no dispute upon this point. From this point, however, men immediately diverge. Much disputation is maintained as to the best way of applying and controlling the labor element. By some it is assumed that labor is available only in connection with capital—that nobody labors, unless somebody else, owning capital, somehow, by the use of that capital, induces him to do it. Having assumed this, they proceed to consider whether it is best that capital shall *hire* laborers, and thus induce them to work by their own consent; or *buy* them, and drive them to it without their consent. Having proceeded so far they naturally conclude that all laborers are necessarily either *hired* laborers, or *slaves*. They further assume that whoever is once a *hired* laborer, is fatally fixed in that condition for life; and thence again that his condition is as bad as, or worse than that of a slave. This is the "*mud-sill*" theory.[50]

But another class of reasoners hold the opinion that there is no *such* relation between capital and labor, as assumed; and that there is no such thing as a freeman being fatally fixed for life, in the condition of a hired laborer, that both these assumptions are false, and all inferences from them groundless. They hold that labor is prior to, and independent of, capital; that, in fact, capital is the fruit of labor, and could never have existed if labor had not *first* existed—that labor can exist without capital, but that capital could never have existed without labor. Hence they hold that labor is the superior—greatly the superior—of capital.

They do not deny that there is, and probably always will be, *a* relation between labor and capital. The error, as they hold, is in assuming that the *whole* labor of the world exists within that relation. A few men own capital; and that few avoid labor themselves, and with their capital, hire, or buy, another few to labor for them. A large majority belong to neither class—neither work for others, nor have others working for them. Even in all our slave States, except South Carolina, a majority of the whole people of all colors, are neither slaves nor masters. In these Free States, a large majority are neither *hirers* nor *hired*. Men, with their families—wives, sons and daughters—work for themselves, on their farms, in their houses and in their shops, taking the whole product to themselves, and asking no favors of capital on the one hand, nor of hirelings or slaves on the other. It is not forgotten that a considerable number of persons mingle their own labor with capital; that is, labor with their own hands, and also buy slaves or hire freemen to labor for them; but this is only a *mixed*, and not a *distinct* class. No principle stated is disturbed by the existence of this mixed class. Again, as has already been said, the opponents of the "*mud-sill*" theory insist that there is not, of necessity, any such thing as the free hired laborer being fixed to that condition for life. There is demonstration for saying this. Many independent men, in this assembly, doubtless a few years ago were hired laborers. And their case is almost if not quite the general rule.

The prudent, penniless beginner in the world, labors

for wages awhile, saves a surplus with which to buy tools or land, for himself; then labors on his own account another while, and at length hires another new beginner to help him.[51] This, say its advocates, is *free* labor—the just and generous, and prosperous system, which opens the way for all—gives hope to all, and energy, and progress, and improvement of condition to all. If any continue through life in the condition of the hired laborer, it is not the fault of the system, but because of either a dependent nature which prefers it, or improvidence, folly, or singular misfortune. . . . Some of you will be successful, and such will need but little philosophy to take them home in cheerful spirits; others will be disappointed, and will be in a less happy mood. To such, let it be said, "Lay it not too much to heart." Let them adopt the maxim, "Better luck next time"; and then, by renewed exertion, make that better luck for themselves.

ADDRESS AT COOPER INSTITUTE, NEW YORK CITY,
February 27, 1860

Mr. President and Fellow-Citizens of New-York. . . . In his speech last autumn, at Columbus, Ohio, as reported in *The New-York Times*, Senator Douglas said: "Our fathers, when they framed the Government under which we live, understood this question just as well, and even better, than we do now."[52]

I fully indorse this, and I adopt it as a text for this discourse. I so adopt it because it furnishes a precise and an agreed starting point for a discussion between Republicans and that wing of the Democracy headed by Senator Douglas. It simply leaves the inquiry: "What was the understanding those fathers had of the question mentioned?"

What is the frame of Government under which we live?

The answer must be: "The Constitution of the United States." That Constitution consists of the original, framed in 1787 (and under which the present government first went into operation), and twelve subsequently framed amendments, the first ten of which were framed in 1789.

Who were our fathers that framed the Constitution? I suppose the "thirty-nine" who signed the original instrument may be fairly called our fathers who framed that part of the present Government. . . . I take these "thirty-nine" . . . as being "our fathers who framed the Government under which we live."

What is the question which, according to the text, those fathers understood "just as well, and even better, than we do now"?

It is this: Does the proper division of local from federal authority, or anything in the Constitution, forbid our *Federal Government* to control as to slavery in *our Federal Territories*?

Upon this, Senator Douglas holds the affirmative, and Republicans the negative. This affirmation and denial form an issue; and this issue—this question—is precisely what the text declares our fathers understood "better than we."

Let us now inquire whether the "thirty-nine," or any of them, ever acted upon this question; and if they did, how they acted upon it—how they expressed that better understanding? . . . We have twenty-three out of our thirty-nine fathers "who framed the Government under which we live," who have, upon their official responsibility and their corporal oaths, acted upon the very question which the text affirms they "understood just as well, and even better, than we do now"; and twenty-one of them—a clear majority of the whole "thirty-nine"—so acting upon it as to make them guilty of gross political impropriety and willful perjury, if, in their understanding, any proper division between local and federal authority, or anything in the Constitution they had made themselves, and sworn to support, forbade the Federal Government to control as to slavery in the federal territories.

. . . But, so far, I have been considering the understanding of the question manifested by the framers of the original Constitution. In and by the original instrument, a mode was provided for amending it; and, as I have already stated, the present frame of "the Government under which we live" consists of that original, and twelve amendatory articles framed and adopted since. Those who now insist that federal control of slavery in federal territories violates the Constitution, point us to the provisions which they suppose it thus violates; and, as I understand, they all fix upon provisions in these amendatory articles, and not in the original instrument. The Supreme Court, in the Dred Scott case, plant themselves upon the fifth amendment, which provides that no person shall be deprived of "life, liberty or property without due process of law"; while Senator Douglas and his peculiar adherents plant themselves upon the tenth amendment, providing that "the powers not delegated to the United States by the Constitution," "are reserved to the States respectively, or to the people."

Now, it so happens that these amendments were framed by the first Congress which sat under the

Constitution—the identical Congress which passed the act already mentioned, enforcing the prohibition of slavery in the Northwestern Territory. Not only was it the same Congress, but they were the identical, same individual men who, at the same session, and at the same time within the session, had under consideration, and in progress toward maturity, these Constitutional amendments, and this act prohibiting slavery in all the territory the nation then owned. The Constitutional amendments were introduced before, and passed after the act enforcing the Ordinance of '87; so that, during the whole pendency of the act to enforce the Ordinance, the Constitutional amendments were also pending. . . . Is it not a little presumptuous in any one at this day to affirm that the two things which that Congress deliberately framed, and carried to maturity at the same time, are absolutely inconsistent with each other?

. . . I go a step further. I defy anyone to show that any living man in the whole world ever did, prior to the beginning of the present century (and I might almost say prior to the beginning of the last half of the present century), declare that, in his understanding, any proper division of local from federal authority, or any part of the Constitution, forbade the Federal Government to control as to slavery in the federal territories. To those who now so declare, I give, not only "our fathers who framed the Government under which we live," but with them all other living men within the century in which it was framed, among whom to search, and they shall not be able to find the evidence of a single man agreeing with them.

. . . But enough! *Let all who believe that "our fathers, who framed the Government under which we live, understood this question just as well, and even better, than we do now," speak as they spoke, and act as they acted upon it. This is all Republicans ask—all Republicans desire—in relation to slavery. As those fathers marked it, so let it be again marked, as an evil not to be extended, but to be tolerated and protected only, because of and so far as its actual presence among us makes that toleration and protection a necessity. Let all the guaranties those fathers gave it, be, not grudgingly, but fully and fairly maintained.* For this Republicans contend, and with this, so far as I know or believe, they will be content.

And now, if they would listen—as I suppose they will not—I would address a few words to the Southern people.

I would say to them: You consider yourselves a reasonable and a just people; and I consider that in the general qualities of reason and justice you are not inferior to any other people. Still, when you speak of us Republicans, you do so only to denounce us as reptiles, or, at the best, as no better than outlaws. You will grant a hearing to pirates or murderers, but nothing like it to "Black Republicans." . . . You say we are sectional. We deny it. That makes an issue; and the burden of proof is upon you. You produce your proof; and what is it? Why, that our party has no existence in your section—gets no votes in your section. The fact is substantially true; but does it prove the issue? If it does, then in case we should, without change of principle, begin to get votes in your section, we should thereby cease to be sectional. You cannot escape this conclusion; and yet, are you willing to abide by it? If you are, you will probably soon find that we have ceased to be sectional, for we shall get votes in your section this very year.

. . . But you say you are conservative—eminently conservative—while we are revolutionary, destructive, or something of the sort. What is conservatism? Is it not adherence to the old and tried, against the new and untried? We stick to, contend for, the identical old policy on the point in controversy which was adopted by "our fathers who framed the Government under which we live"; while you with one accord reject, and scout, and spit upon that old policy, and insist upon substituting something new. True, you disagree among yourselves as to what that substitute shall be. You are divided on new propositions and plans, but you are unanimous in rejecting and denouncing the old policy of the fathers. Some of you are for reviving the foreign slave trade; some for a Congressional Slave-Code for the Territories; some for Congress forbidding the Territories to prohibit Slavery within their limits; some for maintaining Slavery in the Territories through the judiciary; some for the "gurreat pur-rinciple" that "if one man would enslave another, no third man should object," fantastically called "Popular Sovereignty"; but never a man among you in favor of federal prohibition of slavery in federal territories, according to the practice of "our fathers who framed the Government under which we live."

. . . You charge that we stir up insurrections among your slaves. We deny it; and what is your proof? Harper's Ferry! John Brown![53] John Brown was no Republican; and you have failed to implicate a single Republican in his Harper's Ferry enterprise. If any member of our party is guilty in that matter, you know it or you do not know it. If you do know it, you are inexcusable for not designating the man and proving the fact. If you do not know it, you are inexcusable for asserting it, and especially for persisting in the assertion after you have tried and failed to make the proof. You need not be told that persisting in a charge which one does not know to be true, is simply malicious slander.

Some of you admit that no Republican designedly aided or encouraged the Harper's Ferry affair; but still insist that our doctrines and declarations necessarily lead to such results. We do not believe it. We know we hold to no doctrine, and make no declaration, which were not held to and made by "our fathers who framed the Government under which we live." . . . True, we do, in common with "our fathers, who framed the Government under which we live," declare our belief that slavery is wrong; but the slaves do not hear us declare even this. For anything we say or do, the slaves would scarcely know there is a Republican party. . . . Slave insurrections are no more common now than they were before the Republican party was organized. What induced the Southampton insurrection,[54] twenty-eight years ago, in which, at least, three times as many lives were lost as at Harper's Ferry? You can scarcely stretch your very elastic fancy to the conclusion that Southampton was "got up by Black Republicanism."

John Brown's effort was peculiar. It was not a slave insurrection. It was an attempt by white men to get up a revolt among slaves, in which the slaves refused to participate. In fact, it was so absurd that the slaves, with all their ignorance, saw plainly enough it could not succeed. That affair, in its philosophy, corresponds with the many attempts, related in history, at the assassination of kings and emperors. An enthusiast broods over the oppression of a people till he fancies himself commissioned by Heaven to liberate them. He ventures the attempt, which ends in little else than his own execution. Orsini's attempt on Louis Napoleon,[55] and John Brown's attempt at Harper's Ferry were, in their philosophy, precisely the same.

. . . Perhaps you will say the Supreme Court has decided the disputed Constitutional question in your favor. Not quite so. But waiving the lawyer's distinction between dictum and decision,[56] the Court have decided the question for you in a sort of way. The Court have substantially said, it is your Constitutional right to take slaves into the federal territories, and to hold them there as property. When I say the decision was made in a sort of way, I mean it was made in a divided Court, by a bare majority of the Judges,[57] and they not quite agreeing with one another in the reasons for making it. . . . An inspection of the Constitution will show that the right of property in a slave is not "*distinctly* and *expressly* affirmed" in it. . . . But you will not abide the election of a Republican President! In that supposed event, you say, you will destroy the Union; and then, you say, the great crime of having destroyed it will be upon us! That is cool. A highwayman holds a pistol to my ear, and mutters through his teeth, "Stand and deliver, or I shall kill you, and then you will be a murderer!"

. . . A few words now to Republicans. *It is exceedingly desirable that all parts of this great Confederacy shall be at peace, and in harmony, one with another. Let us Republicans do our part to have it so. Even though much provoked, let us do nothing through passion and ill temper. Even though the southern people will not so much as listen to us, let us calmly consider their demands, and yield to them if, in our deliberate view of our duty, we possibly can.* Judging by all they say and do, and by the subject and nature of their controversy with us, let us determine, if we can, what will satisfy them.

. . . The question recurs, what will satisfy them? . . . This, and this only: cease to call slavery *wrong*, and join them in calling it *right*. And this must be done thoroughly—done in *acts* as well as in *words*. Silence will not be tolerated—we must place ourselves avowedly with them . . . suppressing all declarations that slavery is wrong, whether made in politics, in presses, in pulpits, or in private. We must arrest and return their fugitive slaves with greedy pleasure. We must pull down our Free State constitutions. The whole atmosphere must be disinfected from all taint of opposition to slavery, before they will cease to believe that all their troubles proceed from us.

. . . Wrong as we think slavery is, we can yet afford to let it alone where it is, because that much is due to the necessity arising from its actual presence in the nation; but can we, while our votes will prevent it, allow it to spread into the National Territories, and to overrun us here in these Free States? If our sense of duty forbids this, then let us stand by our duty, fearlessly and effectively. Let us be diverted by none of those sophistical contrivances wherewith we are so industriously plied and belabored—contrivances such as groping for some middle ground between the right and the wrong, vain as the search for a man who should be neither a living man nor a dead man—such as a policy of "don't care" on a question about which all true men do care such as Union appeals beseeching true Union men to yield to disunionists, reversing the divine rule, and calling, not the sinners, but the righteous to repentance[58]—such as invocations to Washington, imploring men to unsay what Washington said, and undo what Washington did.

Neither let us be slandered from our duty by false accusations against us, nor frightened from it by menaces of destruction to the Government nor of dungeons to ourselves. LET US HAVE FAITH THAT RIGHT MAKES MIGHT, AND IN THAT FAITH, LET US, TO THE END, DARE TO DO OUR DUTY AS WE UNDERSTAND IT.

SPEECH AT NEW HAVEN, CONNECTICUT,
March 6, 1860

Mr. President and Fellow-Citizens of New Haven: If the Republican party of this nation shall ever have the national house entrusted to its keeping, it will be the duty of that party to attend to all the affairs of national housekeeping. . . . The old question of tariff—a matter that will remain one of the chief affairs of national housekeeping to all time—the question of the management of financial affairs; the question of the disposition of the public domain—how shall it be managed for the purpose of getting it well settled, and of making there the homes of a free and happy people—these will remain open. . . . Yet . . . whether we will or not, the question of Slavery is *the* question, the all absorbing topic of the day. . . .

. . . Look at the magnitude of this subject! One sixth of our population, in round numbers—not quite one sixth, and yet more than a seventh, about one sixth of the whole population of the United States are slaves! The owners of these slaves consider them property. The effect upon the minds of the owners is that of property, and nothing else—it induces them to insist upon all that will favorably affect its value as property, to demand laws and institutions and a public policy that shall increase and secure its value, and make it durable, lasting and universal. The effect on the minds of the owners is to persuade them that there is no wrong in it. The slaveholder does not like to be considered a mean fellow, for holding that species of property, and hence he has to struggle within himself and sets about arguing himself into the belief that Slavery is right. . . . Whether the owners of this species of property do really see it as it is, it is not for me to say, but if they do, they see it as it is through 2,000,000,000 of dollars, and that is a pretty thick coating.

. . . But here in Connecticut and at the North slavery does not exist, and we see it through no such medium. To us it appears natural to think that slaves are human beings; *men*, not property; that some of the things, at least, stated about men in the Declaration of Independence apply to them as well as to us. I say, we think, most of us, that this Charter of Freedom applies to the slave as well as to ourselves, that the class of arguments put forward to batter down that idea, are also calculated to break down the very idea of a free government, even for white men, and to undermine the very foundations of free society. We think Slavery a great moral wrong, and while we do not claim the right to touch it where it exists, we wish to treat it as a wrong in the Territories, where our votes will reach it. We think that a respect for ourselves, a regard for future generations and for the God that made us, require that we put down this wrong where our votes will properly reach it. We think that species of labor an injury to free white men—in short, we think Slavery a great moral, social and political evil, tolerable only because, and so far as its actual existence makes it necessary to tolerate it, and that beyond that, it ought to be treated as a wrong.

. . . Whenever this question shall be settled, it must be settled on some philosophical basis. No policy that does not rest upon some philosophical public opinion can be permanently maintained. And hence, there are but two policies in regard to Slavery that can be at all maintained. The first, based on the property view that slavery is right, conforms to that idea throughout, and demands that we shall do everything for it that we ought to do if it were right. We must sweep away all opposition, for opposition to the right is wrong; we must agree that Slavery is right, and we must adopt the idea that property has persuaded the owner to believe— that Slavery is morally right and socially elevating. This gives a philosophical basis for a permanent policy of encouragement.

The other policy is one that squares with the idea that Slavery is wrong, and it consists in doing everything that we ought to do if it is wrong. Now, I don't wish to be misunderstood, nor to leave a gap down to be misrepresented, even. I don't mean that we ought to attack it where it exists. . . . If I saw a venomous snake crawling in the road, any man would say I might seize the nearest stick and kill it; but if I found that snake in bed with my children, that would be another question. I might hurt the children more than the snake, and it might bite them. Much more, if I found it in bed with my neighbor's children, and I had bound myself by a solemn compact not to meddle with his children under any circumstances, it would become me to let that particular mode of getting rid of the gentleman alone. But if there was a bed newly made up, to which the children were to be taken, and it was proposed to take a batch of young snakes and put them there with them, I take it no man would say there was any question how I ought to decide!

That is just the case! The new territories are the newly made bed to which our children are to go, and it lies with the nation to say whether they shall have snakes mixed up with them or not.

. . . You are ready to say it cannot, but be not too fast! Remember what a long stride has been taken since the repeal of the Missouri Compromise! Do you know of any Democrat, of either branch of the party—do you know one who declares that he believes that the Declaration of Independence has any application to the negro? Judge Taney declares that it has not, and Judge Douglas even vilifies me personally and scolds me roundly for saying that the Declaration applies to all men, and that negroes are men. . . . Four or five years ago we all thought negroes were men, and that when "all men" were named, negroes were included. But *the whole Democratic party has deliberately taken negroes from the class of men and put them in the class of brutes.* Turn it as you will, it is simply the truth! Don't be too hasty then in saying that the people cannot be brought to this new doctrine, but note that long stride.

. . . What we want, and all we want, is to have with us the men who think slavery wrong. But those who say they hate slavery, and are opposed to it, but yet act with the Democratic party—where are they? Let us apply a few tests. You say that you think slavery is wrong, but you denounce all attempts to restrain it. Is there anything else that you think wrong, that you are not willing to deal with as a wrong? Why are you so careful, so tender of this one wrong and no other?

. . . When men are framing a supreme law and chart of government, to secure blessings and prosperity to untold generations yet to come, they use language as short and direct and plain as can be found, to express their meaning. In all matters but this of Slavery the framers of the Constitution used the very clearest, shortest, and most direct language. But the Constitution alludes to Slavery three times without mentioning it once! The language used becomes ambiguous, roundabout, and mystical. They speak of the "immigration of persons," and mean the importation of slaves, but do not say so. In establishing a basis of representation they say "all other persons," when they mean to say slaves—why did they not use the shortest phrase? In providing for the return of fugitives they say "persons held to service or labor." If they had said slaves it would have been plainer, and less liable to misconstruction. Why didn't they do it? We cannot doubt that it was done on purpose. Only one reason is possible, and that is supplied us by one of the framers of the Constitution—and it is not possible for man to conceive of any other—they expected and desired that the system would come to an end, and meant that when it did, the Constitution should not show that there ever had been a slave in this good free country of ours!

. . . *I am glad to see that a system of labor prevails in New England under which laborers* CAN *strike when they want to,* where they are not obliged to work under all circumstances, and are not tied down and obliged to labor whether you pay them or not! I *like* the system which lets a man quit when he wants to, and wish it might prevail everywhere. One of the reasons why I am opposed to Slavery is just here. What is the true condition of the laborer? I take it that it is best for all to leave each man free to acquire property as fast as he can. Some will get wealthy. I don't believe in a law to prevent a man from getting rich; it would do more harm than good. So while we do not propose any war upon capital, we do wish to allow the humblest man an equal chance to get rich with everybody else. When one starts poor, as most do in the race of life, free society is such that he knows he can better his condition; he knows that there is no fixed condition of labor, for his whole life. I am not ashamed to confess that twenty-five years ago I was a hired laborer, mauling rails, at work on a flat-boat—just what might happen to any poor man's son. I want every man to have the chance—and I believe a black man is entitled to it—in which he *can* better his condition—when he may look forward and hope to be a hired laborer this year and the next, work for himself afterward, and finally to hire men to work for him! That is the true system. Up here in New England, you have a soil that scarcely sprouts black-eyed beans, and yet where will you find wealthy men so wealthy, and poverty so rarely in extremity? There is not another such place on earth! I desire that if you get too thick here, and find it hard to better your condition on this soil, you may have a chance to strike and go somewhere else, where you may not be degraded, nor have your family corrupted by forced rivalry with negro slaves. I want you to have a clean bed, and no snakes in it! Then you can better your condition, and so it may go on and on in one ceaseless round so long as man exists on the face of the earth!

. . . If Slavery is right, all words, acts, laws, and Constitutions against it, are themselves wrong, and should be silenced, and swept away. If it is right, we cannot justly object to its nationality[59]—its universality; if it is wrong, they cannot justly insist upon its extension—its enlargement. All they ask, we could readily grant, if we thought slavery right; all we ask, they could as readily grant, if they thought it wrong. Their thinking it right, and our thinking it wrong, is the precise fact upon which depends the whole controversy. Thinking it right as they do, they are not to blame for desiring its full recognition, as being right; but, thinking it wrong, as we do, can we yield to them? Can we cast our votes with their view, and against our own? In view of our moral, social, and political responsibilities, can we do this?

ADDRESS TO THE NEW JERSEY STATE
SENATE, TRENTON, NEW JERSEY,
February 21, 1861

Mr. President and Gentlemen of the Senate of the State of New-Jersey: I am very grateful to you for the honorable reception of which I have been the object. I cannot but remember the place that New-Jersey holds in our early history. In the early Revolutionary struggle, few of the States among the old Thirteen had more of the battle-fields of the country within their limits than old New-Jersey. May I be pardoned if, upon this occasion, I mention that away back in my childhood, the earliest days of my being able to read, I got hold of a small book, such a one as few of the younger members have ever seen, Weems' *Life of Washington*.[60] I remember all the accounts there given of the battle-fields and struggles for the liberties of the country, and none fixed themselves upon my imagination so deeply as the struggle here at Trenton, New-Jersey. The crossing of the river; the contest with the Hessians; the great hardships endured at that time, all fixed themselves on my memory more than any single revolutionary event; and you all know, for you have all been boys, how these early impressions last longer than any others. I recollect thinking then, boy even though I was, that there must have been something more than common that those men struggled for. I am exceedingly anxious that, that thing which they struggled for; that something even more than National Independence; that something that held out a great promise to all the people of the world to all time to come; I am exceedingly anxious that this Union, the Constitution, and the liberties of the people shall be perpetuated in accordance with the original idea for which that struggle was made, and I shall be most happy indeed if I shall be an humble instrument in the hands of the Almighty, and of this, his almost chosen people, for perpetuating the object of that great struggle. . . .

SPEECH AT INDEPENDENCE HALL, PHILADELPHIA, PENNSYLVANIA,
February 22, 1861

I am filled with deep emotion at finding myself standing here in the place where were collected together the wisdom, the patriotism, the devotion to principle, from which sprang the institutions under which we live. You have kindly suggested to me that in my hands is the task of restoring peace to our distracted country. I can say in return, sir, that all the political sentiments I entertain have been drawn, so far as I have been able to draw them, from the sentiments which originated, and were given to the world from this hall in which we stand. I have never had a feeling politically that did not spring from the sentiments embodied in the Declaration of Independence. I have often pondered over the dangers which were incurred by the men who assembled here and adopted that Declaration of Independence—I have pondered over the toils that were endured by the officers and soldiers of the army, who achieved that Independence. I have often inquired of myself, what great principle or idea it was that kept this Confederacy so long together. It was not the mere matter of the separation of the colonies from the mother land; but something in that Declaration giving liberty, not alone to the people of this country, but hope to the world for all future time. It was that which gave promise that in due time the weights should be lifted from the shoulders of all men, and that *all* should have an equal chance. This is the sentiment embodied in that Declaration of Independence.

Now, my friends, can this country be saved upon that basis? If it can, I will consider myself one of the happiest men in the world if I can help to save it. If it can't be saved upon that principle, it will be truly awful. But, if this country cannot be saved without giving up that principle—I was about to say I would rather be assassinated on this spot than to surrender it. Now, in my view of the present aspect of affairs, there is no need of bloodshed and war. There is no necessity for it. I am not in favor of such a course, and I may say in advance, there will be no blood shed unless it be forced upon the Government. The Government will not use force unless force is used against it.

. . . My friends, this is a wholly unprepared speech. I did not expect to be called upon to say a word when I came here—I supposed I was merely to do something towards raising a flag. I may, therefore, have said something indiscreet, but I have said nothing but what I am willing to live by, and, in the pleasure of Almighty God, die by.

FIRST INAUGURAL ADDRESS, WASHINGTON, DC,
March 4, 1861

Fellow-Citizens of the United States:

In compliance with a custom as old as the government itself, I appear before you to address you briefly, and to take, in your presence, the oath prescribed by the Constitution of the United States, to be taken by the President "before he enters on the execution of his office."

. . . Apprehension seems to exist among the people of the Southern States, that by the accession of a Republican administration, their property, and their peace, and personal security, are to be endangered. There has never been any reasonable cause for such apprehension. Indeed, the most ample evidence to the contrary has all the while existed, and been open to their inspection. It is found in nearly all the published speeches of him who now addresses you. . . . I add too, that all the protection which, consistently with the Constitution and the laws, can be given, will be cheerfully given to all the States when lawfully demanded, for whatever cause—as cheerfully to one section, as to another.

There is much controversy about the delivering up of fugitives from service or labor. . . . There is some difference of opinion whether this clause should be enforced by national or by state authority; but surely that difference is not a very material one. If the slave is to be surrendered, it can be of but little consequence to him, or to others, by which authority it is done. And should any one, in any case, be content that his oath shall go unkept, on a merely unsubstantial controversy as to *how* it shall be kept?

Again, in any law upon this subject, ought not all the safeguards of liberty known in civilized and humane jurisprudence to be introduced, so that a free man be not, in any case, surrendered as a slave? And might it not be well, at the same time, to provide by law for the enforcement of that clause in the Constitution which guaranties that "The citizens of each State shall be entitled to all privileges and immunities of citizens in the several States"?

I take the official oath today, with no mental reservations, and with no purpose to construe the Constitution or laws, by any hypercritical rules. . . . I now enter upon the same task for the brief constitutional term of four years, under great and peculiar difficulty. A disruption of the Federal Union heretofore only menaced, is now formidably attempted.

I hold, that in contemplation of universal law, and of the Constitution, the Union of these States is perpetual. Perpetuity is implied, if not expressed, in the fundamental law of all national governments. It is safe to assert that no government proper, ever had a provision in its organic law for its own termination. Continue to execute all the express provisions of our national Constitution, and the Union will endure forever—it being impossible to destroy it, except by some action not provided for in the instrument itself.

Again, if the United States be not a government proper, but an association of States in the nature of contract merely, can it, as a contract, be peaceably unmade, by less than all the parties who made it? One party to a contract may violate it—break it, so to speak; but does it not require all to lawfully rescind it?

Descending from these general principles, we find the proposition that, in legal contemplation, the Union

is perpetual, confirmed by the history of the Union itself. The Union is much older than the Constitution. It
was formed in fact, by the Articles of Association in
1774. It was matured and continued by the Declaration
of Independence in 1776. It was further matured and
the faith of all the then thirteen States expressly plighted
and engaged that it should be perpetual, by the Articles
of Confederation in 1778. And finally, in 1787, one of
the declared objects for ordaining and establishing the
Constitution, was "*to form a more perfect union.*" But if
destruction of the Union, by one, or by a part only, of the
States, be lawfully possible, the Union is *less* perfect than
before the Constitution, having lost the vital element of
perpetuity.

It follows from these views that no State, upon its
own mere motion, can lawfully get out of the Union—
that *resolves* and *ordinances* to that effect are legally void;
and that acts of violence, within any State or States,
against the authority of the United States, are insurrectionary or revolutionary, according to circumstances.

I therefore consider that, in view of the Constitution
and the laws, the Union is unbroken; and, to the extent
of my ability, I shall take care, as the Constitution itself
expressly enjoins upon me, that the laws of the Union be
faithfully executed in all the States. . . . In doing this
there needs to be no bloodshed or violence; and there
shall be none, unless it be forced upon the national authority. The power confided to me, will be used to hold,
occupy, and possess the property, and places belonging
to the government, and to collect the duties and im-
posts; but beyond what may be necessary for these objects, there will be no invasion—no using of force
against, or among the people anywhere. . . . Will you
hazard so desperate a step, while there is any possibility

that any portion of the ills you fly from, have no real existence? Will you, while the certain ills you fly to, are greater than all the real ones you fly from? Will you risk the commission of so fearful a mistake?

All profess to be content in the Union, if all constitutional rights can be maintained. Is it true, then, that any right, plainly written in the Constitution, has been denied? I think not. . . . Think, if you can, of a single instance in which a plainly written provision of the Constitution has ever been denied. If, by the mere force of numbers, a majority should deprive a minority of any clearly written constitutional right, it might, in a moral point of view, justify revolution—certainly would, if such right were a vital one. But such is not our case. All the vital rights of minorities, and of individuals, are so plainly assured to them, by affirmations and negations, guaranties and prohibition in the Constitution, that controversies never arise concerning them. . . . If a minority, in such case, will secede rather than acquiesce, they make a precedent which, in turn, will divide and ruin them; for a minority of their own will secede from them, whenever a majority refuses to be controlled by such minority.

. . . Plainly, the central idea of secession, is the essence of anarchy. A majority, held in restraint by constitutional checks, and limitations, and always changing easily, with deliberate changes of popular opinions and sentiments, is the only true sovereign of a free people. Whoever rejects it, does, of necessity, fly to anarchy or to despotism. Unanimity is impossible; the rule of a minority, as a permanent arrangement, is wholly inadmissable; so that, rejecting the majority principle, anarchy, or despotism in some form, is all that is left.

I do not forget the position assumed by some, that

constitutional questions are to be decided by the Supreme Court; nor do I deny that such decisions . . . are also entitled to very high respect and consideration, in all parallel cases, by all other departments of the government. . . . At the same time the candid citizen must confess that if the policy of the government, upon vital questions, affecting the whole people, is to be irrevocably fixed by decisions of the Supreme Court, the instant they are made, in ordinary litigation between parties, in personal actions, the people will have ceased, to be their own rulers, having, to that extent, practically resigned their government, into the hands of that eminent tribunal. . . .

Physically speaking, we cannot separate. We cannot remove our respective sections from each other, nor build an impassable wall between them. A husband and wife may be divorced, and go out of the presence, and beyond the reach of each other; but the different parts of our country cannot do this. They cannot but remain face to face; and intercourse, either amicable or hostile, must continue between them. Is it possible then to make that intercourse more advantageous, or more satisfactory, *after* separation than *before*? Can aliens make treaties easier than friends can make laws? Can treaties be more faithfully enforced between aliens, than laws can among friends? Suppose you go to war, you cannot fight always; and when, after much loss on both sides, and no gain on either, you cease fighting, the identical old questions, as to terms of intercourse, are again upon you.

This country, with its institutions, belongs to the people who inhabit it. Whenever they shall grow weary of the existing government, they can exercise their *constitutional* right of amending it, or their *revolutionary* right to dismember, or overthrow it. I cannot be ignorant of the fact that many worthy, and patriotic citizens are desirous of having the national constitution amended. While I make no recommendation of amendments . . . I understand a proposed amendment to the Constitution . . . has passed Congress, to the effect that the federal government, shall never interfere with the domestic institutions of the States, including that of persons held to service. . . . Holding such a provision to now be implied constitutional law, I have no objection to its being made express, and irrevocable.

My countrymen, one and all, think calmly and *well*, upon this whole subject. Nothing valuable can be lost by taking time. If there be an object to *hurry* any of you, in hot haste, to a step which you would never take *deliberately*, that object will be frustrated by taking time; but no good object can be frustrated by it. . . . Intelligence, patriotism, Christianity, and a firm reliance on Him, who has never yet forsaken this favored land, are still competent to adjust, in the best way, all our present difficulty.

In *your* hands, my dissatisfied fellow countrymen, and not in *mine*, is the momentous issue of civil war. The government will not assail *you*. You can have no conflict, without being yourselves the aggressors. *You* have no oath registered in Heaven to destroy the government, while *I* shall have the most solemn one to "preserve, protect and defend" it.

I am loth to close. We are not enemies, but friends. We must not be enemies. Though passion may have strained, it must not break our bonds of affection. The mystic chords of memory, stretching from every battle-field, and patriot grave, to every living heart and hearthstone, all over this broad land, will yet swell the chorus of the Union, when again touched, as surely they will be, by the better angels of our nature.[61]

MESSAGE TO THE SPECIAL SESSION OF
THE 37TH CONGRESS,
WASHINGTON, DC,
July 4, 1861

Fellow-citizens of the Senate and House of Representatives: . . . At the beginning of the present Presidential term, four months ago, the functions of the Federal Government were found to be generally suspended within the several States of South Carolina, Georgia, Alabama, Mississippi, Louisiana, and Florida. . . .[62] Within these States, all the Forts, Arsenals, Dock-yards, Customhouses, and the like, including the movable and stationary property in, and about them, had been seized, and were held in open hostility to this Government, excepting only Forts Pickens, Taylor, and Jefferson, on, and near the Florida coast, and Fort Sumter, in Charleston harbor, South Carolina. . . . An ordinance had been adopted in each of these States, declaring the States, respectively, to be separated from the National Union. A formula for instituting a combined government of these States had been promulgated; and this illegal organization, in the character of confederate States was already invoking recognition, aid, and intervention, from Foreign Powers.

Finding this condition of things, and believing it to be an imperative duty upon the incoming Executive, to prevent, if possible, the consummation of such attempt to destroy the Federal Union, a choice of means to that end became indispensable. This choice was made; and was declared in the Inaugural address. The policy chosen looked to the exhaustion of all peaceful measures, before a resort to any stronger ones. It sought only to hold the public places and property, not already wrested from the

Government, and to collect the revenue; relying for the rest, on time, discussion, and the ballot-box. It promised a continuance of the mails, at government expense, to the very people who were resisting the government; and it gave repeated pledges against any disturbance to any of the people, or any of their rights. Of all that which a president might constitutionally, and justifiably, do in such a case, everything was foreborne, without which, it was believed possible to keep the government on foot.

On the 5th of March (the present incumbent's first full day in office), a letter of Major [Robert] Anderson, commanding at Fort Sumter, written on the 28th of February, and received at the War Department on the 4th of March, was, by that Department, placed in his hands. This letter expressed the professional opinion of the writer, that reinforcements could not be thrown into that Fort within the time for his relief, rendered necessary by the limited supply of provisions, and with a view of holding possession of the same, with a force of less than twenty thousand good, and well-disciplined men. This opinion was concurred in by all the officers of his command; and their *memoranda* on the subject, were made enclosures of Major Anderson's letter. The whole was immediately laid before Lieutenant General [Winfield] Scott, who at once concurred with Major Anderson in opinion. On reflection, however, he took full time, consulting with other officers, both of the Army and the Navy; and, at the end of four days, came reluctantly, but decidedly, to the same conclusion as before. He also stated at the same time that no such sufficient force was then at the control of the Government, or could be raised, and brought to the ground, within the time when the provisions in the Fort would be exhausted. In a purely military point of view, this reduced the duty of the administration, in the case, to the mere matter of getting the garrison safely out of the Fort.

It was believed, however, that to so abandon that position, under the circumstances, would be utterly ruinous; that the *necessity* under which it was to be done, would not be fully understood—that, by many, it would be construed as a part of a *voluntary* policy—that, at home, it would discourage the friends of the Union, embolden its adversaries, and go far to insure to the latter, a recognition abroad—that, in fact, it would be our national destruction consummated. This could not be allowed. Starvation was not yet upon the garrison; and ere it would be reached, *Fort Pickens* might be reinforced. This last, would be a clear indication of *policy*, and would better enable the country to accept the evacuation of Fort Sumter, as a military *necessity*. . . . By the affair at Fort Sumter, with its surrounding circumstances, that point was reached. Then, and thereby, the assailants of the Government, began the conflict of arms, without a gun in sight, or in expectancy, to return their fire, save only the few in the Fort, sent to that harbor, years before, for their own protection, and still ready to give that protection, in whatever was lawful. In this act, discarding all else, they have forced upon the country, the distinct issue: "Immediate dissolution, or blood."

And this issue embraces more than the fate of these United States. It presents to the whole family of man, the question, whether a constitutional republic, or a democracy—a government of the people, by the same people—can, or cannot, maintain its territorial integrity, against its own domestic foes. It presents the question, whether discontented individuals, too few in numbers to control administration, according to organic law, in any case, can always, upon the pretenses made in this case, or on any other pretenses, or arbitrarily, without any pretense, break up their Government, and thus practically put an end to free government upon the earth. It forces us to ask: "Is there, in all republics, this inherent, and fatal weakness? Must a government, of necessity, be too *strong* for the liberties of its own people, or too *weak* to maintain its own existence?"

So viewing the issue, no choice was left but to call out the war power of the Government; and so to resist force, employed for its destruction, by force, for its preservation.

The call was made; and the response of the country was most gratifying; surpassing, in unanimity and spirit, the most sanguine expectation. . . . A call was made for seventy-five thousand militia; and rapidly following this, a proclamation was issued for closing the ports of the insurrectionary districts by proceedings in the nature of Blockade. So far all was believed to be strictly legal. At this point the insurrectionists announced their purpose to enter upon the practice of privateering. Other calls were made for volunteers, to serve three years, unless sooner discharged; and also for large additions to the regular Army and Navy. These measures, whether strictly legal or not, were ventured upon, under what appeared to be a popular demand, and a public necessity; trusting, then as now, that Congress would readily ratify them. It is believed that nothing has been done beyond the constitutional competency of Congress.

Soon after the first call for militia, it was considered a duty to authorize the Commanding General, in proper cases, according to his discretion, to suspend the privilege of the writ of habeas corpus; or, in other words, to arrest, and detain, without resort to the ordinary processes and forms of law, such individuals as he might deem dangerous to the public safety.[63] This authority has purposely been exercised but very sparingly. Nevertheless, the legality and propriety of what has been done under it, are questioned; and the attention of the country has been called to the proposition that one who is sworn to "take care that the laws be faithfully executed," should not himself violate them. Of course some consideration was given to the questions of power, and propriety, before this matter was acted upon. The whole of the laws which were required to be faithfully executed, were being resisted, and failing of execution, in nearly one-third of the States. Must they be allowed to finally fail of execution, even had it been perfectly clear, that by the use of the means necessary to their execution, some single law, made in such extreme tenderness of the citizen's liberty, that practically, it relieves more of the guilty, than of the innocent, should, to a very limited extent, be violated? To state the question more directly, are all the laws, *but one*, to go unexecuted, and the government itself go to pieces, lest that one be violated? Even in such a case, would not the official oath be broken, if the government should be overthrown, when it was believed that disregarding the single law, would tend to preserve it? But it was not believed that this question was presented. It was not believed that any law was violated. The provision of the Constitution that "The privilege of the writ of habeas corpus, shall not be suspended unless when, in cases of rebellion or invasion, the public safety may require it,"[64] is equivalent to a provision—is a provision—that such privilege may be suspended when, in cases of rebellion, or invasion, the public safety *does* require it. It was decided that we have a case of rebellion, and that the public safety does require the qualified suspension of the privilege of the writ which was authorized to be made. Now it is insisted that Congress, and not the Executive, is vested with this power. But the Constitution itself, is silent as to which, or who, is to exercise the power; and as the provision was plainly made for a dangerous emergency, it cannot be believed the framers of the instrument intended, that in every case, the danger should run its course, until Congress could be called together; the very assembling of which might be prevented, as was intended in this case, by the rebellion. . . .

It might seem, at first thought, to be of little difference whether the present movement at the South be called "secession" or "rebellion." The movers, however, well understand the difference. At the beginning, they knew they could never raise their treason to any respectable magnitude, by any name which implies *violation* of law. They knew their people possessed as much of moral sense, as much of devotion to law and order, and as much pride in, and reverence for, the history, and government, of their common country, as any other civilized, and patriotic people. They knew they could make no advancement directly in the teeth of these strong and noble sentiments. Accordingly they commenced by an insidious debauching of the public mind. They invented an ingenious sophism, which, if conceded, was followed by perfectly logical steps, through all the incidents, to the complete destruction of the Union. The sophism itself is, that any state of the Union may, *consistently* with the national Constitution, and therefore *lawfully*, and *peacefully*, withdraw from the Union, without the consent of the Union, or of any other state. The little disguise that the supposed right is to be exercised only for just cause, themselves to be the sole judge of its justice, is too thin to merit any notice.

With rebellion thus sugar-coated, they have been drugging the public mind of their section for more than thirty years; and, until at length, they have brought many good men to a willingness to take up arms against the government the day *after* some assemblage of men have enacted the farcical pretense of taking their State out of the Union, who could have been brought to no such thing the day *before*.

This sophism derives much—perhaps the whole—of its currency, from the assumption that there is some omnipotent, and sacred supremacy, pertaining to a *State*—to each State of our Federal Union. Our States have neither more, nor less power, than that reserved to them, in the Union, by the Constitution—no one of them ever having been a State *out* of the Union. The original ones passed into the Union even *before* they cast off their British colonial dependence; and the new ones each came into the Union directly from a condition of dependence, excepting Texas. And even Texas, in its temporary independence, was never designated a State. . . . The States have their *status* IN the Union, and they have no other *legal status*. If they break from this, they can only do so against law, and by revolution. The Union, and not themselves separately, procured their independence, and their liberty. By conquest, or purchase, the Union gave each of them, whatever of independence, and liberty, it has. The Union is older than any of the States; and, in fact, it created them as States.

Unquestionably the States have the powers, and rights, reserved to them in, and by the National Constitution; but among these, surely, are not included all conceivable powers, however mischievous, or destructive; but, at most, such only, as were known in the world, at the time, as governmental powers; and certainly, a power to destroy the government itself, had never been known as a governmental—as a merely administrative power. This relative matter of national power, and State rights, as a principle, is no other than the principle of *generality*, and *locality*. Whatever concerns the whole, should be confided to the whole—to the general government; while, whatever concerns *only* the State, should be left exclusively, to the State. This is all there is of original principle about it. Whether the national Constitution, in defining boundaries between the two, has applied the principle with exact accuracy, is not to be questioned. We are all bound by that defining, without question.

What is now combatted, is the position that secession is *consistent* with the Constitution—is *lawful*, and *peaceful*. . . . Whoever, in any section, proposes to abandon such a government, would do well to consider, in deference to what principle it is, that he does it—what better he is likely to get in its stead—whether the substitute will give, or be intended to give, so much of good to the people. There are some foreshadowings on this subject. Our adversaries have adopted some declarations of independence; in which, unlike the good old one, penned by Jefferson, they omit the words "all men are created equal." Why? They have adopted a temporary national constitution, in the preamble of which, unlike our good old one, signed by Washington, they omit "We, the People," and substitute "We, the deputies of the sovereign and independent States." Why? Why this deliberate pressing out of view, the rights of men, and the authority of the people?

This is essentially a People's contest. On the side of the Union, it is a struggle for maintaining in the world, that form, and substance of government, whose leading object is, to elevate the condition of men—to lift artificial weights from all shoulders—to clear the paths of laudable pursuit for all—to afford all, an unfettered start, and a fair chance, in the race of life. Yielding to partial, and temporary departures, from necessity, this is the leading object of the government for whose existence we contend.

. . . Our popular government has often been called an experiment. Two points in it, our people have already settled—the successful *establishing*, and the successful *administering* of it. One still remains—its successful *maintenance* against a formidable internal attempt to overthrow it. It is now for them to demonstrate to the world, that those who can fairly carry an election, can also suppress a rebellion—that ballots are the rightful, and peaceful, successors of bullets; and that when ballots have fairly, and constitutionally, decided, there can be no successful appeal, back to bullets; that there can be no successful appeal, except to ballots themselves, at succeeding elections. Such will be a great lesson of peace; teaching men that what they cannot take by an election, neither can they take it by a war—teaching all, the folly of being the beginners of a war. . . .

The Constitution provides, and all the States have accepted the provision, that "The United States shall guarantee to every State in this Union a republican form of government."[65] But, if a State may lawfully go out of the Union, having done so, it may also discard the republican form of government; so that to prevent its going out, is an indispensable *means*, to the *end*, of maintaining the guaranty mentioned; and when an end is lawful and obligatory, the indispensable means to it, are also lawful, and obligatory.

It was with the deepest regret that the Executive found the duty of employing the war power, in defense of the government, forced upon him. He could but perform this duty, or surrender the existence of the government. No compromise, by public servants, could, in this case, be a cure; not that compromises are not often proper, but that no popular government can long survive a marked precedent, that those who carry an election, can only save the government from immediate destruction, by giving up the main point, upon which the people gave the election. . . . The Executive could not have consented that these institutions shall perish; much less could he, in betrayal of so vast, and so sacred a trust, as these free people had confided to him. He felt that he had no moral right to shrink; nor even to count the chances of his own life, in what might follow. In full view of his great responsibility, he has, so far, done what he has deemed his duty. You will now, according to your own judgment, perform yours. He sincerely hopes that your views, and your action, may so accord with his, as to assure all faithful citizens, who have been disturbed in their rights, of a certain, and speedy restoration to them, under the Constitution, and the laws.

And having thus chosen our course, without guile, and with pure purpose, let us renew our trust in God, and go forward without fear, and with manly hearts.

ABRAHAM LINCOLN

FIRST ANNUAL MESSAGE TO
CONGRESS, WASHINGTON, DC,
December 3, 1861

Fellow-Citizens of the Senate and House of Representatives: In the midst of unprecedented political
troubles, we have cause of great gratitude to God for
unusual good health, and most abundant harvests.

. . . Under and by virtue of the act of Congress entitled "An act to confiscate property used for insurrectionary purposes," approved August 6, 1861,[66] the legal
claims of certain persons to the labor and service of certain other persons have become forfeited; and numbers
of the latter, thus liberated, are already dependent on the
United States, and must be provided for in some way.
Besides this, it is not impossible that some of the States
will pass similar enactments for their own benefit respectively, and by operation of which persons of the
same class will be thrown upon them for disposal. In
such case I recommend that Congress provide for ac-
cepting such persons from such States, according to
some mode of valuation, in lieu, *pro tanto*, of direct taxes,
or upon some other plan to be agreed on with such
States respectively; that such persons, on such accep-
tance by the general government, be at once deemed
free; and that, in any event, steps be taken for colonizing
both classes (or the one first mentioned, if the other
shall not be brought into existence) at some place, or
places, in a climate congenial to them. It might be well
to consider, too, whether the free colored people already
in the United States could not, so far as individuals may
desire, be included in such colonization.

To carry out the plan of colonization may involve the
acquiring of territory, and also the appropriation of

money beyond that to be expended in the territorial acquisition. Having practiced the acquisition of territory for nearly sixty years, the question of constitutional power to do so is no longer an open one with us. . . . On this whole proposition—including the appropriation of money with the acquisition of territory, does not the expediency amount to absolute necessity—that, without which the government itself cannot be perpetuated? The war continues. In considering the policy to be adopted for suppressing the insurrection, I have been anxious and careful that the inevitable conflict for this purpose shall not degenerate into a violent and remorseless revolutionary struggle. I have, therefore, in every case, thought it proper to keep the integrity of the Union prominent as the primary object of the contest on our part, leaving all questions which are not of vital military importance to the more deliberate action of the legislature.

In the exercise of my best discretion I have adhered to the blockade of the ports held by the insurgents, instead of putting in force, by proclamation, the law of Congress enacted at the late session, for closing those ports.[67]

So, also, obeying the dictates of prudence, as well as the obligations of law, instead of transcending, I have adhered to the act of Congress to confiscate property used for insurrectionary purposes. If a new law upon the same subject shall be proposed, its propriety will be duly considered.

The Union must be preserved, and hence, all indispensable means must be employed. We should not be in haste to determine that radical and extreme measures, which may reach the loyal as well as the disloyal, are indispensable.

. . . It continues to develop that the insurrection is largely, if not exclusively, a war upon the first principle of popular government—the rights of the people. Conclusive evidence of this is found in the most grave and maturely considered public documents, as well as in the general tone of the insurgents. In those documents we find the abridgement of the existing right of suffrage and the denial to the people of all right to participate in the selection of public officers, except the legislative boldly advocated, with labored arguments to prove that large control of the people in government, is the source of all political evil. Monarchy itself is sometimes hinted at as a possible refuge from the power of the people.

In my present position, I could scarcely be justified were I to omit raising a warning voice against this approach of returning despotism.

It is not needed, nor fitting here, that a general argument should be made in favor of popular institutions; but there is one point, with its connections, not so hackneyed as most others, to which I ask a brief attention. It is the effort to place *capital* on an equal footing with, if not above *labor*, in the structure of government. It is assumed that labor is available only in connection with capital; that nobody labors unless somebody else, owning capital, somehow by the use of it, induces him to labor. This assumed, it is next considered whether it is best that capital shall *hire* laborers, and thus induce them to work by their own consent, or *buy* them, and drive them to it without their consent. Having proceeded so far, it is naturally concluded that all laborers are either *hired* laborers, or what we call slaves. And further it is assumed that whoever is once a hired laborer, is fixed in that condition for life.

Now, there is no such relation between capital and

labor as assumed; nor is there any such thing as a free man being fixed for life in the condition of a hired laborer. Both these assumptions are false, and all inferences from them are groundless.

Labor is prior to, and independent of, capital. Capital is only the fruit of labor, and could never have existed if labor had not first existed. Labor is the superior of capital, and deserves much the higher consideration. Capital has its rights, which are as worthy of protection as any other rights. Nor is it denied that there is, and probably always will be, a relation between labor and capital, producing mutual benefits. The error is in assuming that the whole labor of community exists within that relation. A few men own capital, and that few avoid labor themselves, and, with their capital, hire or buy another few to labor for them. A large majority belong to neither class—neither work for others, nor have others working for them. In most of the southern States, a majority of the whole people of all colors are neither slaves nor masters; while in the northern a large majority are neither hirers nor hired. Men with their families—wives, sons, and daughters—work for themselves, on their farms, in their houses, and in their shops, taking the whole product to themselves, and asking no favors of capital on the one hand, nor of hired laborers or slaves on the other. It is not forgotten that a considerable number of persons mingle their own labor with capital—that is, they labor with their own hands, and also buy or hire others to labor for them; but this is only a mixed, and not a distinct class. No principle stated is disturbed by the existence of this mixed class.

Again: as has already been said, there is not, of necessity, any such thing as the free hired laborer being fixed to that condition for life. Many independent men everywhere in these States, a few years back in their lives, were hired laborers. The prudent, penniless beginner in the world, labors for wages awhile, saves a surplus with which to buy tools or land for himself; then labors on his own account another while, and at length hires another new beginner to help him. This is the just, and generous, and prosperous system, which opens the way to all—gives hope to all, and consequent energy, and progress, and improvement of condition to all. No men living are more worthy to be trusted than those who toil up from poverty—none less inclined to take, or touch, aught which they have not honestly earned. Let them beware of surrendering a political power which they already possess, and which, if surrendered, will surely be used to close the door of advancement against such as they, and to fix new disabilities and burdens upon them, till all of liberty shall be lost. . . . The struggle of today, is not altogether for today—it is for a vast future also. With a reliance on Providence, all the more firm and earnest, let us proceed in the great task which events have devolved upon us.

ABRAHAM LINCOLN

MEMORANDUM OF INTERVIEW WITH JOHN W. CRISFIELD,[68] WASHINGTON, DC, *March 10, 1862*

The President then disclaimed any intent to injure the interests or wound the sensibilities of the slave States. On the contrary, his purpose was to protect the one and respect the other; that we were engaged in a terrible, wasting, and tedious war; immense armies were in the field, and must continue in the field as long as the war lasts; that these armies must, of necessity, be brought into contact with slaves in the States we represented and in other States as they advanced; that slaves would come to the camps and continual irritation was kept up; that he was constantly annoyed by conflicting and antagonistic complaints; on the one side, a certain class complained if the slave was not protected by the army; persons were frequently found who, participating in these views, acted in a way unfriendly to the slaveholder; on the other hand, slaveholders complained that their rights were interfered with, their slaves induced to abscond and protected within the lines; these complaints were numerous, loud, and deep; were a serious annoyance to him and embarrassing to the progress of the war; that it kept alive a spirit hostile to the Government in the States we represented; strengthened the hopes of the Confederates that at some day the border States would unite with them, and thus tend to prolong the war; and he was of opinion, if this resolution[69] should be adopted by Congress and accepted by our States, these causes of irritation and these hopes would be removed, and more would be accomplished towards shortening the war than could be hoped from the greatest victory achieved by Union armies; that he made this proposition in good faith, and desired it to be accepted, if at all, voluntarily, and in the same patriotic spirit in which it was made; that emancipation was a subject exclusively under the control of the States. . . . The proposition now submitted does not encounter any constitutional difficulty. It proposes simply to co-operate with any State by giving such State pecuniary aid; and he thought that the resolution, as proposed by him, would be considered rather as the expression of a sentiment than as involving any constitutional question.

. . . He said he did not pretend to disguise his anti-slavery feeling; that he thought it was wrong and should continue to think so; but that was not the question we had to deal with now. Slavery existed, and that, too, as well by the act of the North as of the South; and in any scheme to get rid of it, the North, as well as the South, was morally bound to do its full and equal share. He thought the institution wrong, and ought never to have existed; but yet he recognized the rights of property which had grown out of it, and would respect those rights as fully as similar rights in any other property; that property can exist, and does legally exist. He thought such a law wrong, but the rights of property resulting must be respected; he would get rid of the odious law, not by violating the right, but by encouraging the proposition and offering inducements to give it up.

APPEAL TO BORDER STATE REPRESENTATIVES TO FAVOR COMPENSATED EMANCIPATION, WASHINGTON, DC, *July 12, 1862*

Gentlemen. After the adjournment of Congress, now very near, I shall have no opportunity of seeing you for several months. Believing that you of the border states hold more power for good than any other equal number of members, I feel it a duty which I cannot justifiably waive, to make this appeal to you. I intend no reproach or complaint when I assure you that in my opinion, if you all had voted for the resolution in the gradual emancipation message of last March, the war would now be substantially ended. And the plan therein proposed is yet one of the most potent, and swift means of ending it. Let the states which are in rebellion see, definitely and certainly, that, in no event, will the states you represent ever join their proposed Confederacy, and they cannot, much longer maintain the contest. But you cannot divest them of their hope to ultimately have you with them so long as you show a determination to perpetuate the institution within your own states. Beat them at elections, as you have overwhelmingly done, and, nothing daunted, they still claim you as their own. You and I know what the lever of their power is. Break that lever before their faces, and they can shake you no more forever.

Most of you have treated me with kindness and consideration; and I trust you will not now think I improperly touch what is exclusively your own, when, for the sake of the whole country I ask, "Can you, for your states, do better than to take the course I urge?" Discarding *punctillio*, and maxims adapted to more manageable times, and looking only to the unprecedentedly stern facts of our case, can you do better in any possible event? You prefer that the constitutional relation of the states to the nation shall be practically restored, without disturbance of the institution; and if this were done, my whole duty, in this respect, under the constitution, and my oath of office, would be performed. But it is not done, and we are trying to accomplish it by war. The incidents of the war cannot be avoided. If the war continue long, as it must, if the object be not sooner attained, the institution in your states will be extinguished by mere friction and abrasion—by the mere incidents of the war. It will be gone, and you will have nothing valuable in lieu of it. Much of its value is gone already. How much better for you, and for your people, to take the step which, at once, shortens the war, and secures substantial compensation for that which is sure to be wholly lost in any other event. How much better to thus save the money which else we sink forever in the war. How much better to do it while we can, lest the war ere long render us pecuniarily unable to do it. How much better for you, as seller, and the nation as buyer, to sell out, and buy out, that without which the war could never have been, than to sink both the thing to be sold, and the price of it, in cutting one another's throats.

I do not speak of emancipation at *once*, but of a *decision* at once to emancipate *gradually*. Room in South America for colonization can be obtained cheaply, and in abundance; and when numbers shall be large enough to be company and encouragement for one another, the freed people will not be so reluctant to go.

. . . You are patriots and statesmen; and, as such, I pray you, consider this proposition; and, at least commend it to the consideration of your states and people. As you would perpetuate popular government for the best people in the world, I beseech you that you do in no wise omit this. Our common country is in great peril, demanding the loftiest views, and boldest action to bring it speedy relief. Once relieved, its form of government is saved to the world; its beloved history, and cherished memories, are vindicated; and its happy future fully assured, and rendered inconceivably grand. To you, more than to any others, the privilege is given, to assure that happiness, and swell that grandeur, and to link your own names therewith forever.

ADDRESS ON COLONIZATION TO AN AFRICAN AMERICAN DELEGATION, WASHINGTON, DC,
August 14, 1862

. . . The President, after a few preliminary observations, informed them that a sum of money had been appropriated by Congress, and placed at his disposition for the purpose of aiding the colonization in some country of the people, or a portion of them, of African descent, thereby making it his duty, as it had for a long time been his inclination, to favor that cause; and why, he asked, should the people of your race be colonized, and where? Why should they leave this country? This is, perhaps, the first question for proper consideration. You and we are different races. We have between us a broader difference than exists between almost any other two races. Whether it is right or wrong I need not discuss, but this physical difference is a great disadvantage to us both, as I think your race suffer very greatly, many of them by living among us, while ours suffer from your presence. In a word we suffer on each side. If this is admitted, it affords a reason at least why we should be separated. . . . Your race are suffering, in my judgment, the greatest wrong inflicted on any people. But even when you cease to be slaves, you are yet far removed from being placed on an equality with the white race. You are cut off from many of the advantages which the other race enjoy. The aspiration of men is to enjoy equality with the best when free, but on this broad continent, not a single man of your race is made the equal of a single man of ours. Go where you are treated the best, and the ban is still upon you.

I do not propose to discuss this, but to present it as a fact with which we have to deal. I cannot alter it if I would. It is a fact, about which we all think and feel alike, I and you. We look to our condition, owing to the existence of the two races on this continent. I need not recount to you the effects upon white men, growing out of the institution of Slavery. I believe in its general evil effects on the white race. See our present condition— the country engaged in war!—our white men cutting one another's throats, none knowing how far it will extend; and then consider what we know to be the truth. But for your race among us there could not be war, although many men engaged on either side do not care for you one way or the other. Nevertheless, I repeat, without the institution of Slavery and the colored race as a basis, the war could not have an existence.

It is better for us both, therefore, to be separated. I know that there are free men among you, who even if they could better their condition are not as much inclined to go out of the country as those, who being slaves could obtain their freedom on this condition. I suppose one of the principal difficulties in the way of colonization is that the free colored man cannot see that his comfort would be advanced by it. . . . This is (I speak in no unkind sense) an extremely selfish view of the case. . . . One reason for an unwillingness to do so is that some of you would rather remain within reach of the country of your nativity. I do not know how much attachment you may have toward our race. It does not strike me that you have the greatest reason to love them. But still you are attached to them at all events.

The place I am thinking about having for a colony is in Central America . . . this particular place has all the advantages for a colony. On both sides there are harbors among the finest in the world. Again, there is evidence of very rich coal mines. A certain amount of coal is valuable in any country, and there may be more than enough for the wants of the country. Why I attach so much importance to coal is, it will afford an opportunity to the inhabitants for immediate employment till they get ready to settle permanently in their homes. . . . We have been mistaken all our lives if we do not know whites as well as blacks look to their self-interest. . . . Besides, I would endeavor to have you made equals, and have the best assurance that you should be the equals of the best.

. . . The practical thing I want to ascertain is whether I can get a number of able-bodied men, with their wives and children, who are willing to go, when I present evidence of encouragement and protection. Could I get a hundred tolerably intelligent men, with their wives and children, to "cut their own fodder," so to speak?[70] Can I have fifty? If I could find twenty-five able-bodied men, with a mixture of women and children, good things in the family relation, I think I could make a successful commencement. I want you to let me know whether this can be done or not. This is the practical part of my wish to see you. . . . I ask you then to consider seriously not pertaining to yourselves merely, nor for your race, and ours, for the present time, but as one of the things, if successfully managed, for the good of mankind. . . .

REPLY TO EMANCIPATION MEMORIAL
PRESENTED BY CHICAGO CHRISTIANS
OF ALL DENOMINATIONS,
WASHINGTON, DC,
September 13, 1862[71]

The subject presented in the memorial is one upon which I have thought much for weeks past, and I may even say for months. I am approached with the most opposite opinions and advice, and that by religious men, who are equally certain that they represent the Divine will. I am sure that either the one or the other class is mistaken in that belief, and perhaps in some respects both. I hope it will not be irreverent for me to say that if it is probable that God would reveal his will to others, on a point so connected with my duty, it might be supposed he would reveal it directly to me; for, unless I am more deceived in myself than I often am, it is my earnest desire to know the will of Providence in this matter. *And if I can learn what it is I will do it!* These are not, however, the days of miracles, and I suppose it will be granted that I am not to expect a direct revelation. I must study the plain physical facts of the case, ascertain what is possible and learn what appears to be wise and right. The subject is difficult, and good men do not agree. For instance, the other day four gentlemen of standing and intelligence . . . from New York called, as a delegation, on business connected with the war; but, before leaving, two of them earnestly beset me to proclaim general emancipation, upon which the other two at once attacked them! You know, also, that the last session of Congress had a decided majority of anti-slavery men, yet they could not unite on this policy. And the same is true of the religious people. Why, the rebel soldiers are praying with a great deal more earnestness, I fear, than our own troops, and expecting God to favor their side; for one of our soldiers, who had been taken prisoner, told [Massachusetts] Senator [Henry] Wilson, a few days since, that he met with nothing so discouraging as the evident sincerity of those he was among in their prayers. But we will talk over the merits of the case.

What *good* would a proclamation of emancipation from me do, especially as we are now situated? I do not want to issue a document that the whole world will see must necessarily be inoperative, like the Pope's bull against the comet![72] Would *my word* free the slaves, when I cannot even enforce the Constitution in the rebel States? Is there a single court, or magistrate, or individual that would be influenced by it there? And what reason is there to think it would have any greater effect upon the slaves than the late law of Congress, which I approved, and which offers protection and freedom to the slaves of rebel masters who come within our lines?[73] Yet I cannot learn that that law has caused a single slave to come over to us. And suppose they could be induced by a proclamation of freedom from me to throw themselves upon us, *what should we do with them?* How can we feed and care for such a multitude?

. . . Understand, I raise no objections against it on legal or constitutional grounds; for, as commander-in-chief of the army and navy, in time of war, I suppose I have a right to take any measure which may best subdue the enemy. Nor do I urge objections of a moral nature, in view of possible consequences of insurrection and massacre at the South. I view the matter as a practical war measure, to be decided upon according to the advantages or disadvantages it may offer to the suppression of the rebellion.

. . . Slavery is the root of the rebellion, or at least its *sine qua non.* The ambition of politicians may have instigated them to act, but they would have been impotent without slavery as their instrument. I will also concede that emancipation would help us in Europe, and convince them that we are incited by something more than ambition. I grant further that it would help *somewhat* at the North, though not so much, I fear, as you and those you represent imagine. Still, some additional strength would be added in that way to the war. And then unquestionably it would weaken the rebels by drawing off their laborers, which is of great importance. But I am not so sure we could do much with the blacks. If we were to arm them, I fear that in a few weeks the arms would be in the hands of the rebels; and indeed thus far we have not had arms enough to equip our white troops. I will mention another thing, though it meet only your scorn and contempt: There are fifty thousand bayonets in the Union armies from the Border Slave States. It would be a serious matter if, in consequence of a proclamation such as you desire, they should go over to the rebels.

. . . Do not misunderstand me, because I have mentioned these objections. They indicate the difficulties that have thus far prevented my action in some such way as you desire. I have not decided against a proclamation of liberty to the slaves, but hold the matter under advisement. And I can assure you that the subject is on my mind, by day and night, more than any other. Whatever shall appear to be God's will I will do. . . .

SECOND ANNUAL MESSAGE TO CONGRESS, WASHINGTON, DC,
December 1, 1862

. . . Without slavery the rebellion could never have existed; without slavery it could not continue. Among the friends of the Union there is great diversity, of sentiment, and of policy, in regard to slavery, and the African race amongst us. Some would perpetuate slavery; some would abolish it suddenly, and without compensation; some would abolish it gradually, and with compensation; some would remove the freed people from us, and some would retain them with us. . . . It is insisted that their presence would injure, and displace white labor and white laborers. If there ever could be a proper time for mere catch arguments, that time surely is not now. In times like the present, men should utter nothing for which they would not willingly be responsible through time and in eternity. Is it true, then, that colored people can displace any more white labor, by being free, than by remaining slaves? If they stay in their old places, they jostle no white laborers; if they leave their old places, they leave them open to white laborers. . . . Thus, the customary amount of labor would still have to be performed; the freed people would surely not do more than their old proportion of it, and very probably, for a time, would do less, leaving an increased part to white laborers, bringing their labor into greater demand, and, consequently, enhancing the wages of it.

. . . But it is dreaded that the freed people will swarm forth, and cover the whole land? Are they not already in the land? Will liberation make them any more numerous? Equally distributed among the whites of the whole country, and there would be but one colored to seven whites. Could the one, in any way, greatly disturb the seven? There are many communities now, having more than one free colored person, to seven whites; and this, without any apparent consciousness of evil from it. The District of Columbia, and the states of Maryland and Delaware, are all in this condition. The District has more than one free colored to six whites; and yet, in its frequent petitions to Congress, I believe it has never presented the presence of free colored persons as one of its grievances. But why should emancipation south, send the free people north? People, of any color, seldom run, unless there be something to run from. . . .

Is it doubted, then, that the plan I propose, if adopted, would shorten the war, and thus lessen its expenditure of money and of blood? Is it doubted that it would restore the national authority and national prosperity, and perpetuate both indefinitely? Is it doubted that we here—Congress and Executive—can secure its adoption? Will not the good people respond to a united, and earnest appeal from us? Can we, can they, by any other means, so certainly, or so speedily, assure these vital objects? We can succeed only by concert. It is not "Can *any* of us *imagine* better?" but "Can we *all* do better?" Object whatsoever is possible, still the question recurs "Can we do better?" The dogmas of the quiet past, are inadequate to the stormy present. The occasion is piled high with difficulty, and we must rise with the occasion. As our case is new, so we must think anew, and act anew. We must disenthrall ourselves, and then we shall save our country.

Fellow-citizens, *we* cannot escape history. We of this Congress and this administration, will be remembered in spite of ourselves. No personal significance, or insignificance, can spare one or another of us. The fiery trial through which we pass, will light us down, in honor or dishonor, to the latest generation. We *say* we are for the Union. The world will not forget that we say this. We know how to save the Union. The world knows we do know how to save it. We—even *we here*—hold the power, and bear the responsibility. In *giving* freedom to the *slave*, we *assure* freedom to the *free*—honorable alike in what we give, and what we preserve. We shall nobly save, or meanly lose, the last best, hope of earth. Other means may succeed; this could not fail. The way is plain, peaceful, generous, just—a way which, if followed, the world will forever applaud, and God must forever bless.

ABRAHAM LINCOLN

LETTER TO JAMES C. CONKLING,[74] WASHINGTON, DC, *August 26, 1863*

Your letter inviting me to attend a mass-meeting of unconditional Union men, to be held at the capital of Illinois, on the 3rd day of September, has been received.

. . . There are those who are dissatisfied with me. To such I would say: You desire peace; and you blame me that we do not have it. But how can we attain it? There are but three conceivable ways. First, to suppress the rebellion by force of arms. This, I am trying to do. Are you for it? If you are, so far we are agreed. If you are not for it, a second way is, to give up the Union. I am against this. Are you for it? If you are, you should say so plainly. If you are not for *force*, nor yet for *dissolution*, there only remains some imaginable *compromise*. I do not believe any compromise, embracing the maintenance of the Union, is now possible. All I learn, leads to a directly opposite belief. The strength of the rebellion, is its military—its army. That army dominates all the country, and all the people, within its range. Any offer of terms made by any man or men within that range, in opposition to that army, is simply nothing for the present; because such man or men, have no power whatever to enforce their side of a compromise, if one were made with them. . . . No paper compromise, to which the controllers of Lee's army are not agreed, can, at all, affect that army.[75]

. . . But, to be plain, you are dissatisfied with me about the negro. Quite likely there is a difference of opinion between you and myself upon that subject. I certainly wish that all men could be free, while I suppose you do not. Yet I have neither adopted, nor proposed any measure, which is not consistent with even your view, provided you are for the Union. I suggested compensated emancipation; to which you replied you wished not to be taxed to buy negroes. But I had not asked you to be taxed to buy negroes, except in such way, as to save you from greater taxation to save the Union exclusively by other means.

You dislike the emancipation proclamation; and, perhaps, would have it retracted. You say it is unconstitutional—I think differently. I think the constitution invests its commander-in-chief, with the law of war, in time of war. The most that can be said, if so much, is, that slaves are property. Is there—has there ever been any question that by the law of war, property, both of enemies and friends, may be taken when needed? And is it not needed whenever taking it, helps us, or

hurts the enemy? Armies, the world over, destroy enemies' property when they can not use it; and even destroy their own to keep it from the enemy. Civilized
belligerents do all in their power to help themselves, or
hurt the enemy, except a few things regarded as barba-
rous or cruel. Among the exceptions are the massacre of
vanquished foes, and non-combatants, male and female.

But the proclamation, as law, either is valid, or is not
valid. If it is not valid, it needs no retraction. If it is valid,
it cannot be retracted, any more than the dead can be
brought to life. Some of you profess to think its retraction would operate favorably for the Union. Why better
after the retraction, than *before* the issue? . . . The war has
certainly progressed as favorably for us, since the issue
of the proclamation as before. I know as fully as one can
know the opinions of others, that some of the com-
manders of our armies in the field who have given us our
most important successes, believe the emancipation
policy, and the use of colored troops, constitute the
heaviest blow yet dealt to the rebellion; and that, at least
one of those important successes, could not have been
achieved when it was, but for the aid of black soldiers.
. . . You say you will not fight to free negroes. Some
of them seem willing to fight for you; but, no matter.
Fight you, then, exclusively to save the Union. I issued
the proclamation on purpose to aid you in saving the
Union. Whenever you shall have conquered all resistance to the Union, if I shall urge you to continue fighting, it will be an apt time, then, for you to declare you
will not fight to free negroes.

I thought that in your struggle for the Union, to
whatever extent the negroes should cease helping the
enemy, to that extent it weakened the enemy in his resistance to you. Do you think differently? I thought that

whatever negroes can be got to do as soldiers, leaves just so much less for white soldiers to do, in saving the Union. Does it appear otherwise to you? But negroes, like other people, act upon motives. Why should they do anything for us, if we will do nothing for them? If they stake their lives for us, they must be prompted by the strongest motive even the promise of freedom. And the promise being made, must be kept.

The signs look better. The Father of Waters again goes unvexed to the sea. Thanks to the great North-West for it. Nor yet wholly to them. Three hundred miles up, they met New England, Empire, Keystone, and Jersey, hewing their way right and left. The sunny South too, in more colors than one, also lent a hand. On the spot, their part of the history was jotted down in black and white. The job was a great national one; and let none be banned who bore an honorable part in it. And while those who have cleared the great river may well be proud, even that is not all. It is hard to say that anything has been more bravely, and well done, than at Antietam, Murfreesboro, Gettysburg, and on many fields of lesser note. Nor must Uncle Sam's Web-feet be forgotten. At all the watery margins they have been present. Not only on the deep sea, the broad bay, and the rapid river, but also up the narrow muddy bayou, and wherever the ground was a little damp, they have been, and made their tracks. Thanks to all. For the great republic—for the principle it lives by, and keeps alive—for man's vast future,—thanks to all.

Peace does not appear so distant as it did. I hope it will come soon, and come to stay; and so come as to be worth the keeping in all future time. It will then have been proved that, among free men, there can be no successful appeal from the ballot to the bullet; and that they who take such appeal are sure to lose their case, and pay the cost. And then, there will be some black men who can remember that, with silent tongue, and clenched teeth, and steady eye, and well-poised bayonet, they have helped mankind on to this great consummation; while, I fear, there will be some white ones, unable to forget that, with malignant heart, and deceitful speech, they have strove to hinder it.

Still let us not be over-sanguine of a speedy final triumph. Let us be quite sober. Let us diligently apply the means, never doubting that a just God, in his own good time, will give us the rightful result. Yours very truly

A. LINCOLN.

ADDRESS DELIVERED AT THE DEDICATION OF THE CEMETERY AT GETTYSBURG, *November 19, 1863*

Four score and seven years ago our fathers brought forth on this continent, a new nation, conceived in Liberty, and dedicated to the proposition that all men are created equal.

Now we are engaged in a great civil war, testing whether that nation, or any nation so conceived and so dedicated, can long endure. We are met on a great battle-field of that war. We have come to dedicate a portion of that field, as a final resting place for those who here gave their lives that that nation might live. It is altogether fitting and proper that we should do this.

But, in a larger sense, we cannot dedicate—we cannot

consecrate—we cannot hallow—this ground. The brave men, living and dead, who struggled here, have consecrated it, far above our poor power to add or detract. The world will little note, nor long remember what we say here, but it can never forget what they did here. It is for us the living, rather, to be dedicated here to the unfinished work which they who fought here have thus far so nobly advanced. It is rather for us to be here dedicated to the great task remaining before us—that from these honored dead we take increased devotion to that cause for which they gave the last full measure of devotion—that we here highly resolve that these dead shall not have died in vain—that this nation, under God, shall have a new birth of freedom—and that government of the people, by the people, for the people, shall not perish from the earth.

ABRAHAM LINCOLN

TO ALBERT G. HODGES,[76]
WASHINGTON, DC,
April 4, 1864

My dear Sir: You ask me to put in writing the substance of what I verbally said the other day, in your presence, to [Kentucky] Governor [Thomas E.] Bramlette and Senator [Archibald] Dixon. It was about as follows:

"I am naturally anti-slavery. If slavery is not wrong, nothing is wrong. I cannot remember when I did not so think, and feel. And yet I have never understood that the Presidency conferred upon me an unrestricted right to act officially upon this judgment and feeling. It was in the oath I took that I would, to the best of my ability, preserve, protect, and defend the Constitution of the United States. I could not take the office without taking the oath. Nor was it my view that I might take an oath to get power, and break the oath in using the power. I understood, too, that in ordinary civil administration this oath even forbade me to practically indulge my primary abstract judgment on the moral question of slavery. I had publicly declared this many times, and in many ways. And I aver that, to this day, I have done no official act in mere deference to my abstract judgment and feeling on slavery. I did understand however, that my oath to preserve the Constitution to the best of my ability, imposed upon me the duty of preserving, by every indispensable means, that government—that nation—of which that Constitution was the organic law. Was it possible to lose the nation, and yet preserve the Constitution? By general law life and limb must be protected; yet often a limb must be amputated to save a life; but a life is never wisely given to save a limb. I felt that measures, otherwise unconstitutional, might become lawful, by becoming indispensable to the preservation of the Constitution, through the preservation of the nation. Right or wrong, I assumed this ground, and now avow it. I could not feel that, to the best of my ability, I had even tried to preserve the Constitution, if, to save slavery, or any minor matter, I should permit the wreck of government, country, and Constitution all together. . . . When, in March, and May, and July 1862 I made earnest, and successive appeals to the border states to favor compensated emancipation, I believed the indispensable necessity for military emancipation, and arming the blacks would come, unless averted by that measure. They declined the proposition; and I was, in my best judgment, driven to the alternative of either surrendering the Union, and with it, the Constitution, or of laying strong hand upon the colored element. I chose the latter. In choosing it, I hoped for greater gain than loss; but of this, I was not entirely confident. More than a year of trial now shows no loss by it in our foreign relations, none in our home popular sentiment, none in our white military force—no loss by it anyhow or anywhere. On the contrary, it shows a gain of quite a hundred and thirty thousand soldiers, seamen, and laborers. These are palpable facts, about which, as facts, there can be no cavilling. We have the men; and we could not have had them without the measure.

"And now let any Union man who complains of the measure, test himself by writing down in one line that he is for subduing the rebellion by force of arms; and in the next, that he is for taking these hundred and thirty thousand men from the Union side, and placing them where they would be but for the measure he condemns. If he cannot face his case so stated, it is only because he cannot face the truth."

SPEECH TO THE ONE HUNDRED SIXTY-SIXTH OHIO REGIMENT,[77] WASHINGTON, DC, *August 22, 1864*

I suppose you are going home to see your families and friends. For the service you have done in this great struggle in which we are engaged I present you sincere thanks for myself and the country. I almost always feel inclined, when I happen to say anything to soldiers, to impress upon them in a few brief remarks the importance of success in this contest. It is not merely for to-day, but for all time to come that we should perpetuate for our children's children this great and free government, which we have enjoyed all our lives. I beg you to remember this, not merely for my sake, but for yours. I happen temporarily to occupy this big White House. I am a living witness that any one of your children may look to come here as my father's child has. It is in order that each of you may have through this free government which we have enjoyed, an open field and a fair chance for your industry, enterprise and intelligence; that you may all have equal privileges in the race of life, with all its desirable human aspirations. It is for this the struggle should be maintained, that we may not lose our birthright—not only for one, but for two or three years. The nation is worth fighting for, to secure such an inestimable jewel.

RESPONSE TO A SERENADE, WASHINGTON, DC, *November 10, 1864*

It has long been a grave question whether any government, not too strong for the liberties of its people, can be strong enough to maintain its own existence, in great emergencies.

On this point the present rebellion brought our republic to a severe test; and a presidential election occurring in regular course during the rebellion[78] added not a little to the strain. If the loyal people, *united*, were put to the utmost of their strength by the rebellion, must they not fail when *divided*, and partially paralyzed, by a political war among themselves?

But the election was a necessity. We cannot have free government without elections; and if the rebellion could force us to forego, or postpone a national election, it might fairly claim to have already conquered and ruined us. The strife of the election is but human nature practically applied to the facts of the case. What has occurred in this case, must ever recur in similar cases. Human nature will not change. In any future great national trial, compared with the men of this, we shall have as weak, and as strong; as silly and as wise; as bad and good. Let us, therefore, study the incidents of this, as philosophy to learn wisdom from, and none of them as wrongs to be revenged.

But the election, along with its incidental, and undesirable strife, has done good too. It has demonstrated that a people's government can sustain a national election, in the midst of a great civil war. Until now it has not been known to the world that this was a possibility. It shows also how *sound*, and how *strong* we still are. It shows that, even among candidates of the same party, he who is most devoted to the Union, and most opposed to treason, can receive most of the people's votes. It shows also, to the extent yet known, that we have more men now, than we had when the war began. Gold is good in its place; but living, brave, patriotic men, are better than gold.

But the rebellion continues; and now that the election is over, may not all, having a common interest, re-unite in a common effort, to save our common country? For my own part I have striven, and shall strive to avoid placing any obstacle in the way. So long as I have

been here I have not willingly planted a thorn in any
man's bosom. . . .[79]

RESPONSE TO A SERENADE,
WASHINGTON, DC,
February 1, 1865

The President said he supposed the passage through
Congress of the Constitutional amendment for the
abolishment of Slavery throughout the United States,
was the occasion to which he was indebted for the honor
of this call. The occasion was one of congratulation to
the country and to the whole world. But there is a task
yet before us—to go forward and consummate by the
votes of the States that which Congress so nobly began
yesterday. He had the honor to inform those present that
Illinois had already to-day done the work.[80] Maryland
was about half through; but he felt proud that Illinois
was a little ahead. He thought this measure was a very
fitting if not an indispensable adjunct to the winding up
of the great difficulty. He wished the reunion of all the
States perfected and so effected as to remove all causes
of disturbance in the future; and to attain this end it was
necessary that the original disturbing cause should, if
possible, be rooted out. He thought all would bear him
witness that he had never shrunk from doing all that he
could to eradicate Slavery by issuing an emancipation
proclamation. But that proclamation falls far short of
what the amendment will be when fully consummated.
A question might be raised whether the proclamation
was legally valid. It might be added that it only aided

those who came into our lines and that it was inoperative as to those who did not give themselves up, or that
it would have no effect upon the children of the slaves
born hereafter. In fact it would be urged that it did not
meet the evil. But this amendment is a King's cure for all
the evils. It winds the whole thing up. He would repeat
that it was the fitting if not indispensable adjunct to the
consummation of the great game we are playing. He
could not but congratulate all present, himself, the country and the whole world upon this great moral victory.

SECOND INAUGURAL ADDRESS, WASHINGTON, DC,
March 4, 1865

At this second appearing to take the oath of the
presidential office, there is less occasion for an extended address than there was at the first. Then a statement, somewhat in detail, of a course to be pursued,
seemed fitting and proper. Now, at the expiration of four
years, during which public declarations have been constantly called forth on every point and phase of the great
contest which still absorbs the attention, and engrosses
the energies of the nation, little that is new could be
presented. The progress of our arms, upon which all else
chiefly depends, is as well known to the public as to
myself; and it is, I trust, reasonably satisfactory and encouraging to all. With high hope for the future, no pre-
diction in regard to it is ventured.

On the occasion corresponding to this four years ago,
all thoughts were anxiously directed to an impending

civil war. All dreaded it—all sought to avert it. While the inaugural address was being delivered from this place, devoted altogether to *saving* the Union without war, insurgent agents were in the city seeking to *destroy* it without war—seeking to dissolve the Union, and divide effects, by negotiation. Both parties deprecated war; but one of them would *make* war rather than let the nation survive; and the other would *accept* war rather than let it perish. And the war came.

One eighth of the whole population were colored slaves, not distributed generally over the Union, but localized in the Southern part of it. These slaves constituted a peculiar and powerful interest. All knew that this interest was, somehow, the cause of the war. To strengthen, perpetuate, and extend this interest was the object for which the insurgents would rend the Union, even by war; while the government claimed no right to do more than to restrict the territorial enlargement of it. Neither party expected for the war, the magnitude, or the duration, which it has already attained. Neither anticipated that the *cause* of the conflict might cease with, or even before, the conflict itself should cease. Each looked for an easier triumph, and a result less fundamental and astounding. Both read the same Bible, and pray to the same God; and each invokes His aid against the other. It may seem strange that any men should dare to ask a just God's assistance in wringing their bread from the sweat of other men's faces; but let us judge not that we be not judged.[81] The prayers of both could not be answered; that of neither has been answered fully. The Almighty has His own purposes. "Woe unto the world because of offences! for it must needs be that offences come; but woe to that man by whom the offence cometh!"[82] If we shall suppose that American Slavery is one of those offences which, in the providence of God, must needs come, but which, having continued through His appointed time, He now wills to remove, and that He gives to both North and South, this terrible war, as the woe due to those by whom the offence came, shall we discern therein any departure from those divine attributes which the believers in a Living God always ascribe to Him? Fondly do we hope—fervently do we pray—that this mighty scourge of war may speedily pass away. Yet, if God wills that it continue, until all the wealth piled by the bond-man's two hundred and fifty years of unrequited toil shall be sunk, and until every drop of blood drawn with the lash, shall be paid by another drawn with the sword, as was said three thousand years ago, so still it must be said "the judgments of the Lord, are true and righteous altogether."[83]

With malice toward none; with charity for all; with firmness in the right, as God gives us to see the right, let us strive on to finish the work we are in; to bind up the nation's wounds; to care for him who shall have borne the battle, and for his widow, and his orphan—to do all which may achieve and cherish a just, and a lasting peace, among ourselves, and with all nations.

ADDRESS ON RECONSTRUCTION, WASHINGTON, DC, *April 11, 1865*

We meet this evening, not in sorrow, but in gladness of heart. The evacuation of Petersburg and Richmond, and the surrender of the principal insurgent army, give hope of a righteous and speedy peace whose joyous expression cannot be restrained.[84] . . . By these recent successes the re-inauguration of the national authority—reconstruction—which has had a large share of thought from the first, is pressed much more closely upon our attention. It is fraught with great difficulty. . . . We all agree that the seceded States, so called, are out of their proper practical relation with the Union; and that the sole object of the government, civil and military, in regard to those States is to again get them into that proper practical relation. I believe it is not only possible, but in fact, easier, to do this, without deciding, or even considering, whether these states have even been out of the Union, than with it. Finding themselves safely at home, it would be utterly immaterial whether they had ever been abroad. Let us all join in doing the acts necessary to restoring the proper practical relations between these states and the Union; and each forever after, innocently indulge his own opinion whether, in doing the acts, he brought the States from without, into the Union, or only gave them proper assistance, they never having been out of it.

The amount of constituency, so to speak, on which the new Louisiana government rests, would be more satisfactory to all, if it contained fifty, thirty, or even twenty thousand, instead of only about twelve thousand, as it does. It is also unsatisfactory to some that the elective franchise is not given to the colored man. I would myself prefer that it were now conferred on the very intelligent, and on those who serve our cause as soldiers. Still the question is not whether the Louisiana government, as it stands, is quite all that is desirable. The question is "Will it be wiser to take it as it is, and help to improve it; or to reject, and disperse it? Can Louisiana be brought into proper practical relation with the Union *sooner* by *sustaining*, or by *discarding* her new State Government?"

. . . If we reject, and spurn them, we do our utmost to disorganize and disperse them. We in effect say to the white men "You are worthless, or worse—we will neither help you, nor be helped by you." To the blacks we say "This cup of liberty which these, your old masters, hold to your lips, we will dash from you, and leave you to the chances of gathering the spilled and scattered contents in some vague and undefined when, where, and how." . . . If, on the contrary, we recognize, and sustain the new government of Louisiana the converse of all this is made true. We encourage the hearts, and nerve the arms of the twelve thousand to adhere to their work, and argue for it, and proselyte for it, and fight for it, and feed it, and grow it, and ripen it to a complete success. The colored man too, in seeing all united for him, is inspired with vigilance, and energy, and daring, to the same end. Grant that he desires the elective franchise, will he not attain it sooner by saving the already advanced steps toward it, than by running backward over them? Concede that the new government of Louisiana is only to what it should be as the egg is to the fowl, we shall sooner have the fowl by hatching the egg than by smashing it?

. . . What has been said of Louisiana will apply generally to other States. And yet so great peculiarities pertain to each state; and such important and sudden changes occur in the same state; and, withal, so new and unprecedented is the whole case, that no exclusive, and inflexible plan can safely be prescribed as to details and collaterals. Such exclusive, and inflexible plan, would surely become a new entanglement. Important principles may, and must, be inflexible.

In the present "*situation*" as the phrase goes, it may be my duty to make some new announcement to the people of the South. I am considering, and shall not fail to act, when satisfied that action will be proper.

NOTES

1 Herndon, in *The Hidden Lincoln, from the Letters and Papers of William H. Herndon*, ed. Emmanuel Hertz (New York: Viking Press, 1938), 191–192; Lincoln, "Remarks to Citizens of Gettysburg, Pennsylvania" (November 18, 1863), in *Collected Works of Abraham Lincoln*, ed. Roy P. Basler et al. (New Brunswick, NJ: Rutgers University Press, 1953), 7:16.

2 "Speech at a Republican Banquet, Chicago, Illinois" (December 10, 1856) and "Speech at Cincinnati, Ohio" (September 17, 1859), in *Collected Works*, 2:385, 3:442; Swett, in *Herndon's Informants: Letters, Interviews, and Statements About Abraham Lincoln*, eds. Rodney O. Davis and Douglas L. Wilson (Urbana: University of Illinois Press, 1998), 636.

3 Mary Cunningham Logan, *Reminiscences of a Soldier's Wife* (New York: Charles Scribner's, 1913), 61–62; Marsh, *Lectures on the English Language* (New York: Charles Scribner, 1859), 276; Kenneth Cmiel, *Democratic Eloquence: The Fight Over Popular Speech in Nineteenth-Century America* (Berkeley: University of California Press, 1990), 114–120; Herndon to Jesse W. Weik (January 6, 1887), in *The Hidden Lincoln*, 132–133; Stuart interview with William Henry Herndon (December 20, 1866), in *Herndon's Informants*, 519.

4 James Herndon to William H. Herndon (May 29, 1865), Dennis Hanks interview with Herndon (December 8, 1865), Abner Y. Ellis statement, and Robert Rutledge to Herndon (November 1, 1866), in *Herndon's Informants*, 16, 105, 170, 384.

5 Kimberly K. Smith, *The Dominion of Voice: Riot, Reason, and Romance in Antebellum Politics* (Lawrence: University Press of Kansas, 1999), 93, 107–109; Robert G. Gunderson, "The

Southern Whigs," in *Oratory in the Old South, 1828–1860*, eds.
Waldo W. Braden et al. (Baton Rouge: Louisiana State University Press, 1970), 127–128; Michael P. Kramer, *Imagining Language in America: From the Revolution to the Civil War* (Princeton, NJ: Princeton University Press, 1992), 114; "Congressional Eloquence," *North American Review* 52 (January 1841), 112.

6 Lincoln, "To James C. Conkling" (August 20 and 27, 1863), in *Collected Works*, 6:399, 414; "The Great Union Mass Meeting," *Illinois State Journal* (September 4, 1863).

7 Sumner to Lot M. Morrill, June 15, 1865, in *The Selected Letters of Charles Sumner*, ed. Beverly W. Palmer (Boston: Northeastern University Press, 1990), 2:306.

8 "It is said that every man has his portion of ambition. . . . My only ambition is to do my duty in this world as I am capable of performing it and to merit the good opinion of all man" (George Washington to David Humphreys, *Humphreys' Life of General Washington*, ed. R. Zagarri [Athens: University of Georgia Press, 1991], 47).

9 Daniel Stone was born in Monkton, Vermont, graduated in 1818 from Middlebury College, and practiced law in Ohio before moving to Illinois in 1833. He was one of the "Long Nine" Whigs who, along with Lincoln, represented Sangamon county in the Illinois legislature for 1836–38, but did not serve out his full term, being appointed judge of the Sixth Judicial Circuit (1836–42). He moved again, to Westfield, New Jersey, where he died in 1860 (*Catalogue of the Officers and Alumni of Middlebury College* [Middlebury, VT: The Register Co., 1890], 46).

10 Francis L. McIntosh, a free mulatto steward on the Mississippi steamboat *Flora*, stabbed a St. Louis deputy sheriff to death after the sheriff, George Hammond, attempted to arrest two disorderly boat hands on August 26, 1836. McIntosh was arrested, but dragged from the city jail and burned to death.

11 Lincoln is referring here to the murder on November 7, 1837, of the abolitionist editor Elijah P. Lovejoy of Alton, Illinois, who was killed in a shoot-out with a mob after the press of his newspaper, the *Alton Observer*, had been repeatedly thrown into the Mississippi River.

12 After President Andrew Jackson vetoed the rechartering of

the Second Bank of the United States, federal funds were deposited in a variety of state banks. In an effort to curb abuses in the state banks, President Van Buren backed the creation of a Sub-Treasury within the Department of the Treasury to act as a bank of deposit for federal funds.

13 Stephen Arnold Douglas (he later dropped the second "s") was Lincoln's chief Democratic rival in Illinois politics, and was matched against Lincoln for the senior Illinois U.S. Senate seat in 1858, and for the presidency of the United States in 1860.

14 Locofoco was the name of a popular brand of match, but became the term applied to the most radical faction of the Democratic party in the 1830s after one of their meetings was disrupted by having the gaslights at their meeting turned off by their opponents. The meeting was continued by lighting matches.

15 Hard coin, as opposed to paper bank notes issued by a national bank or individual state banks.

16 It was long believed that scrofula ("the king's evil"), a tubercular infection of the lymph glands, could be cured by the physical touch of royalty.

17 The dog is turned to his own vomit again; and the sow that was washed to her wallowing in the mire (2 Peter 2:22).

18 James Knox Polk.

19 The so-called "Spot Resolutions," introduced by Lincoln on the floor of the House of Representatives on December 22, 1847, demanding that President Polk show "Whether the spot of soil on which the blood of our citizens was shed" actually belonged to the United States (*Congressional Globe*, 30th Congress, 1st Session, 64).

20 The Texan Revolution of 1835–36.

21 Pennsylvania Democratic representative David Wilmot offered an amendment to the appropriations bill for concluding the Mexican War, which stipulated "that, as an express and fundamental condition to the acquisition of any territory from the Republic of Mexico . . . neither slavery nor involuntary servitude shall ever exist in any part of said territory, except for crime . . ." (*Congressional Globe*, 29th Congress, 1st Session, 1217).

22 Representative Alfred Iverson (1798–1873).

23 Andrew Jackson's estate east of Nashville, Tennessee.

24 Brigadier General William Hull surrendered the garrison and fort of Detroit to British forces during the War of 1812; Cass was an officer in Hull's command, but had been sent out of Detroit to reopen Hull's communications, and found on his return that Hull had included him in the surrender agreement.

25 A major American victory of the War of 1812, which took place on October 5, 1813.

26 Indignant at being included by Hull in the surrender of Detroit, Cass broke his sword rather than turn it over to the British, as wartime protocol required.

27 The Black Hawk War began in 1832 when Sauk and Fox Indians under Black Hawk attempted to regain tribal lands they had ceded by treaty in Illinois; Lincoln served as captain of the New Salem militia company that was called out to confront Black Hawk.

28 On May 14, 1832, during the Black Hawk War, Major Isaiah Stillman and his command were routed by Sauk and Fox Indians.

29 The "Free Soil" Party was a short-lived coalition party, composed of antislavery Whigs and Democrats who opposed any further extension of slavery in the western territories. Free-Soilers ran Martin Van Buren for president in 1848, and John P. Hale in 1852. They never won more than 10 percent of the popular vote, but Lincoln feared that they would siphon off enough Whig votes to throw the 1848 election to Lewis Cass, the Democratic candidate.

30 The Missouri Compromise (1819–21), the Nullification Controversy (1832), and the Compromise of 1850.

31 "An Act to Organize the Territories of Kansas and Nebraska" (May 30, 1854), in *Statutes at Large and Treaties of the United States of America*, from December 1, 1851, to March 3, 1855, 33rd Congress, 1st Session, ed. George Minot (Boston: Little, Brown, 1855), 277–290.

32 "As far as it goes."

33 *Hamlet*, act 3, scene 3. This occurs immediately after Lincoln's favorite speech from *Hamlet*, that of the King, "Oh, my offense is rank."

34 For out of the abundance of the heart the mouth speaketh (Luke 6:45).

35 Lincoln is quoting from a protest that originally appeared in the *London Daily News* (September 12, 1854) and was re-printed in American newspapers, denouncing the appoint-ment of a Louisiana slaveholder, Pierre Soule, as American minister to Madrid. The protest concluded that slavery, "the one retrograde institution in America is undermining the principle of progress, and fatally vitiating the noblest political system that the world ever saw."

36 "Cancel and tear to pieces that great bond" (*Macbeth*, act 3, scene 2).

37 Her children arise up, and call her blessed (Proverbs 31:28).

38 Every kingdom divided against itself is brought to desolation; and every city or house divided against itself shall not stand (Matthew 12:25).

39 Stephen A. Douglas, as the chair of the Committee on Terri-tories, introduced the Kansas-Nebraska Bill on January 4, 1854.

40 Franklin Pierce announced, in his final annual message to Congress, that "in the progress of constitutional inquiry and reflection it had now at length come to be seen clearly that Congress does not possess constitutional power to impose restrictions of this character upon any present or future State of the Union" (Pierce, "Fourth Annual Message," December 2, 1856, in *A Compilation of the Messages and Papers of the Presi-dents*, ed. James D. Richardson [Washington, DC: Bureau of National Literature and Art, 1907], 5:401).

41 James Buchanan, in his inaugural address, affirmed that "A difference of opinion has arisen in regard to the point of time when the people of a Territory shall decide this question for themselves. This is, happily . . . a judicial question, which le-gitimately belongs to the Supreme Court of the United States, before whom it is now pending, and will, it is understood, be speedily and finally settled. To their decision, in common with all good citizens, I shall cheerfully submit, whatever this may be" ("Inaugural Address," in *A Compilation of the Messages and Papers of the Presidents*, 7:2962).

42 March 6, 1857.

43 The "Lecompton Constitution" was a pro-slavery territorial constitution written for Kansas in November 1847. Buchanan recommended adoption of the Lecompton Constitution in his first annual message to Congress on December 8, 1857.

44 In defending popular sovereignty on the floor of the Senate,

Douglas declared that "If Kansas wants a slave-State constitution she has a right to it. . . . I do not care whether it is voted down or voted up" (Douglas, "The President's Message," December 9, 1857, *Congressional Globe*, 35th Congress, 1st session, 18).

45 Chief Justice Taney wrote, "It is absolutely certain that the African race were not included under the name of citizens of a State . . . and that they are not included, and were not intended to be included, under the word 'citizens' in the Constitution, and can therefore claim none of the rights and privileges which that instrument provides for and secures to citizens of the United States" (*A Report of the Decision of the Supreme Court of the United States and the Opinion of the Judges Thereof, in the Case of Dred Scott versus John F. A. Sandford, December Term, 1856*, Benjamin C. Howard, compiler [New York: D. Appleton, 1857], 404).

46 In other words, Stephen A. Douglas, Franklin Pierce, Roger B. Taney, and James Buchanan.

47 For to him that is joined to all the living there is hope: for a living dog is better than a dead lion (Ecclesiastes 9:4).

48 Be ye therefore perfect, even as your Father which is in heaven is perfect (Matthew 5:48).

49 "And damn'd be him that first cries, 'Hold, enough!'" (*Macbeth*, act 5, scene 8).

50 In a speech on March 4, 1858, James Henry Hammond (U.S. Senator from South Carolina) declared that every society requires a "mud-sill" class to perform the menial labor which ensured the leisure and civilization of the upper classes. Hammond argued for the superiority of Southern slave-holding society to Northern free labor, since in the South enslaved blacks formed the "mud-sill," while in the free North, white laborers were degraded to performing the "mud-sill" tasks (*Congressional Globe*, 35th Congress, 1st Session, 962).

51 "To begin as hired labourers, then after a few years to work on their own account, and finally employ others, is the normal condition of labourers in a new country . . . like America or Australia" (J. S. Mill, "On the Probable Futurity of the Labouring Classes," in *Principles of Political Economy*, with some of their "Application to Social Philosophy," in *Collected Works of John Stuart Mill*, 3:766–767).

52 "Speech of Senator Douglas at Columbus, Ohio," *The New York Times* (September 8, 1858); Douglas's overall views were summed-up in "The Dividing Line Between Federal and Local Authority: Popular Sovereignty in the Territories," *Atlantic Monthly* 19 (September 1859), 519–537.

53 The radical abolitionist John Brown staged an armed raid on the Federal Arsenal and Armory at Harpers Ferry, Virginia, on October 16–18, 1859, with a view to securing weapons he would use as part of a general slave uprising. Ten of Brown's raiders, however, were killed and seven captured by U.S. Marines and Virginia militia. Brown himself was hanged at Charlestown, Virginia, on December 8, 1859.

54 The Nat Turner Insurrection, August 21–23, 1831. Turner was hanged on November 11, 1831.

55 On January 14, 1858, the Italian revolutionary Felice Orsini attempted to assassinate the French emperor, Napoleon III, with a bomb.

56 According to the conventions of *stare decisis* ("let the decision stand"), a dictum is a nonbinding opinion, whereas a decision established a precedent that must be incorporated into subsequent decisions.

57 Six of the nine justices of the Taney Court agreed with the ruling in *Dred Scott v. Sanford*; Justice Samuel Nelson concurred with the ruling but objected to the legal reasoning involved, whereas Justices Benjamin Curtis and John McLean dissented.

58 I am not come to call the righteous, but sinners to repentance (Matthew 9:13).

59 That is, nationalization.

60 Mason Locke "Parson" Weems (1759–1825), author of *The Life of Washington* (1800).

61 "The better angel is a man right fair" (Shakespeare, Sonnet 144).

62 South Carolina was the first state to secede from the Union, on December 20, 1860, followed by Mississippi (January 9, 1861), Florida (January 10, 1861), Alabama (January 11, 1861), Georgia (January 19, 1861), Louisiana (January 26, 1861), and Texas (February 1, 1861).

63 On April 27, 1861, Lincoln authorized Lt.-Gen. Winfield Scott to arrest saboteurs along the rail corridor from Wash-

ington to Philadelphia and to suspend the writ of habeas corpus to prevent any attempt by the civil courts to reclaim them from military custody. The family of one of those arrested, John Merryman of Cockeysville, Maryland, and a lieutenant in the Maryland Home Guard, appealed to Chief Justice Taney for a writ of habeas corpus. When the commandant at Ft. McHenry, Gen. George Cadwalader, refused to respond to Taney's writ, Taney wrote a blistering opinion, denouncing Lincoln's suspension, in *ex parte Merryman*.

64 Article 1, section 9.

65 Article 4, section 4.

66 *The Statutes-at-Large, Treaties and Proclamations of the United States of America*, from December 5, 1859, to March 3, 1863, ed. George P. Sanger (Boston: Little, Brown, 1863), 319.

67 Lincoln issued a proclamation of blockade on April 19, 1861, followed by a supplemental proclamation on April 27.

68 John W. Crisfield (1806–1897) was a congressman from Maryland.

69 On March 6, 1862, Lincoln recommended for adoption by both houses of Congress a joint resolution offering federal aid to the border states to fund state initiatives for emancipation.

70 Lincoln may have been referring to Henry Hiram Riley's *The Puddleford Papers: Or, Humors of the West* (1857), a series of humorous sketches where this phrase appears as a description of settlers "who came in when the country was new, and have cut their own fodder ever since" (123).

71 On September 7, 1862, a "public meeting of Christians of all denominations" deputized William Weston Patton (1821–1889; pastor of the First Congregational Church in Chicago and author of *Slavery and Infidelity*, 1856) and John Dempster (1794–1863, a Methodist minister and president of the Garrett Biblical Institute) to present Lincoln with a "memorial in favor of national emancipation." Patton and Dempster submitted a written report of their interview with Lincoln on September 19, 1862, which was followed three days later by the Preliminary Emancipation Proclamation.

72 Lincoln is referring to the apocryphal story of Pope Callixtus III issuing a bill against Halley's comet in 1456.

73 The second Confiscation Act, which Lincoln signed on July 17, 1862.

74 James Cook Conkling (1816–1899) was a longtime acquaintance and political ally of Lincoln's in Springfield, Illinois.

75 Robert E. Lee's Army of Northern Virginia.

76 Albert Gallatin Hodges (1802–1881) was a Kentucky Unionist and editor of the *Frankfort Commonwealth*.

77 The 166th Ohio Volunteer Infantry regiment was a unit of the Ohio National Guard, mobilized for one hundred days' service on May 13, 1864, and sent to Washington to reinforce the garrison of the capital; they were officially mustered out on September 9, 1864.

78 Lincoln was reelected to a second term on November 8, 1864.

79 "Leave her to heaven and to those thorns that in her bosom lodge" (*Hamlet*, act 1, scene 5).

80 Illinois ratified the 13th Amendment on February 1; Maryland ratified on February 3.

81 Judge not, that ye be not judged (Matthew 7:1).

82 Matthew 18:7.

83 Psalm 19:9.

84 Petersburg and Richmond fell to Lt.-Gen. Ulysses S. Grant on April 3, 1865.